INCANDESCENCE

Light Shed through the Word

INCANDESCENCE

Light Shed through the Word

BEN WITHERINGTON III

With an introductory essay by

J. Ellsworth Kalas

WILLIAM B. EERDMANS PUBLISHING COMPANY
GRAND RAPIDS, MICHIGAN / CAMBRIDGE, U.K.

© 2006 Wm. B. Eerdmans Publishing Co.
All rights reserved

Wm. B. Eerdmans Publishing Co.
255 Jefferson Ave. S.E., Grand Rapids, Michigan 49503 /
P.O. Box 163, Cambridge CB3 9PU U.K.

Printed in the United States of America

11 10 09 08 07 06   7 6 5 4 3 2 1

Library of Congress Cataloging-in-Publication Data

Witherington, Ben, 1951–
Incandescence: light shed through the Word / Ben Witherington III;
with an introductory essay by J. Ellsworth Kalas.
p.   cm.
ISBN-10: 0-8028-3208-3 / ISBN-13: 978-0-8028-3208-5 (pbk.: alk. paper)
1. Church year sermons. 2. Sermons, American — 20th century. 3. Preaching.
I. Kalas, J. Ellsworth, 1923–   II. Title.
BV4253.W58   2006
252 — dc22

2006003741

www.eerdmans.com

[Homileticians] should not be governed by their desires. It is impossible to acquire this power except by these two qualities: contempt of praise and the force of eloquence. If either is lacking, the one left is made useless by the divorce from the other. If a preacher despises praise yet does not produce the kind of teaching which is "with grace, seasoned with salt," he is despised by the people, and his sublime words accomplish nothing. And if he is eloquent but a slave to the sound of applause, again an equal damage threatens both him and the people, because through his passion for praise he aims to speak more for the pleasure than the profit of his hearers.

John Chrysostom, *On the Priesthood* 5.2

Contents

CONTENTS

EPIPHANY
The Light Appears

LENT
The Lengthening of the Light

HOLY WEEK AND EASTERTIDE
The Light Rises

Contents

PENTECOST
The Light Bursts into Flame

KINGDOM TIDE
The Dying of the Light

Preface

Many of those for whom I have been writing books over the course of the last twenty-five years have asked me for a collection of my sermons. This is a first effort at honoring that request. Sermons are of course one part Word and one part Spirit, and sometimes it is difficult to get a sense of the aural effect simply by reading a sermon. You lose the cadence, rhythm, and rhetoric of the sermon. But at least if you read what Dr. J. D. Walt, the dean of our chapel at Asbury, says in the following few pages, you may have a sense of the impact crater left by the oral preaching of these sermons.

The other problem with just reading sermons is that it is not always clear what the spiritual impact is intended to be. For this reason Julie Robertson has provided us with spiritual formation guides at the end of each major section of this work. I am very thankful that my Arkansas and Asbury friends J. D. and Julie would help make this a project more user-friendly for the local church and its clergy.

I hope and trust that what is found in this volume will be food for the soul, will lift the spirits, but also, as C. H. Dodd used to say, will tease the mind into active thought. Solid biblical preaching, based on careful and meticulous exegesis and theologizing, is rare in our day, and I do not profess to have completely mastered the art. These sermons should be seen, then, for what they are — efforts that are growing toward the light, all the while attempting to shed a little light.

I am delighted that my colleague and friend Dr. J. Ellsworth Kalas has graciously agreed to provide the essay which immediately follows this preface and the reflections of J. D. Walt, delving into the nature of effective "biblical preaching," a phrase that sadly has almost become an oxymoron in our era. I am honored that so fine a homiletician and teacher of preaching would enrich this volume in this way.

I have chosen the title *Incandescence* for this collection with reason. It is my hope that it will be illuminating, indeed that it will leave those who have engaged with this material luminous at a deep level, on fire with the Spirit that prompted these offerings in the first place and stirred up to convict, convince, and convert others. This is the effect of good sermonizing. May the words of these pages and the meditations in our hearts be acceptable in the sight of God, our Rock and Redeemer.

BEN WITHERINGTON III
Pentecost 2005

Incandescence: Some Introductory Reflections

In•can•des•cence
n.
1. The emission of visible light by a hot object.
2. The light emitted by an incandescent object.
3. A high degree of emotion, intensity, or brilliance.

The American Heritage Dictionary

See also:
A bush on fire yet not being consumed.
Jars of clay radiating with the treasure of light.

Our family ends each day with a time of benediction. We offer spoken blessings to one another as a last act of worship before bed. Recently I gave David, our five-year-old, this blessing: "David, may the Holy Spirit fill you so full of the Love of Jesus that you have the power to heal." Then I said, "David, will you give me a blessing?" He sleepily replied, "Dad! I don't know any!" "Come on, David," I said, "I could use a blessing." A flash of light streamed from his eye through the dark room as he said, "Okay, Daddy. You're full of God and light is coming out!"

That's the story of these sermons by my friend Ben Witherington III: incandescence.

> For it is the God who said, "Let light shine out of darkness," who has shone in our hearts to give the light of the knowledge of the glory of God in the face of Jesus Christ. But we have this treasure in clay jars, so that it may be made clear that this extraordinary power belongs to God and does not come from us. (2 Corinthians 4:6-7)

I don't claim to know much about preaching or preachers, but I know them when I see them. And I see a lot of preachers. As the Dean of the Chapel of Asbury Theological Seminary, I listen to a minimum of three sermons a week, and that doesn't include the ones I hear in church on Sunday. I have had the privilege of hearing a number of the sermons in this volume in the vast mix of our seminary's worship life. Permit me a few brief observations on how I've encountered them.

Back up to that word, *encounter*. For my money, the best preaching is an encounter with God. In an age of "teachy" (and sometimes tacky!) sermon outlines and "fill-in-the-blank" preachers, people long for preaching that causes them to look up, to see something beyond the next point. The best preaching has a way of turning one's ears into eyes. One of the marks of good preaching is "visual quality." In other words, as I'm listening to this sermon, *am I seeing anything?* Ben has a way of bringing words together such that they kindle into flame. I've distilled a working definition of preaching from his homiletical practice: Preaching is words emitting Light illuminating Life.

Tucked in the middle of the magnum opus of the Psalms, Psalm 119, the psalmist offers, "The unfolding of your words gives light. It gives understanding to the simple" (v. 130). Surely preaching was not designed to be a series of points to ponder (or, worse, predict), or a mass of content to be mastered. Preaching is an event, an encounter with the living God, an unfolding of Light. The appropriate posture is not pensive note-taking but leaning forward. These sermons unfold the Bible's words in ways emitting Light illuminating Life. They don't leave us with pithy points to remember; rather, they extend our memory of the Story of God by giving us a live encounter with the God of the Story.

A second observation about preaching, preachers, and these sermons: the best ones confront subversively. First we see the light and only later do we begin to notice the shape of our own shadow. I am most drawn to the practices of Jesus on the road to Emmaus. He comes alongside distraught disciples, asks them questions, and begins to unfold the story of

Scripture, revealing the depths of authorial intent. The encounter extends beyond the conversation to table fellowship where his identity is revealed to them in the breaking of the bread: "They said to each other, 'Were not our hearts burning within us while he was talking with us on the road, while he was opening the scriptures to us?'" (Luke 24:32). Ben is a storyteller par excellence and yet he tells stories in service of *the* Story. His storytelling subverts the elaborate and deceptive security systems of the human mind by engaging the heart.

In his book *The Living Reminder: Service and Prayer in Memory of Jesus Christ,* Henri Nouwen captures this mode of storytelling with the following:

> One of the remarkable qualities of the story is that it creates space. We can dwell in a story, walk around, find our own place. The story confronts but does not oppress; the story inspires but does not manipulate. The story invites us to an encounter, a dialog, a mutual sharing. The story brings us into touch with the vision and so guides us. (pp. 65-66)

These sermons engage the intellect, certainly, but not for the sake of increasing knowledge. Ben's preaching makes knowledge the servant of Wisdom, teaching the heart to think and the mind to feel, inspiring and equipping us to live in Christ with skill. It is said of John Wesley's sermons that they inspired conversion long after the preaching was over, as people gathered together in smaller groups to conference. These sermons work in the same fashion. In the encounter we are swept up into beholding the Light of the World. Only after the fact do we realize its piercing force. This Light always reveals the contrast of dimness and elucidates the distortions of our shadow. It does so not through focusing us on ourselves but through showing us something infinitely more beautiful.

A final word. One of the Wesley brothers, on being asked why so many people came out to hear him preach, responded something to the effect of, "I set myself on fire and people come to watch me burn." Anyone who witnesses the preaching of Ben Witherington III will see something of the same phenomenon. It's why a book of sermons can never do preaching justice. Ben is "full of God and Light is coming out!" You get a feel for that in reading these sermons, but they are no substitute for the live article. I close by expressing my gratitude for this man who is a servant of the Church, a preacher's preacher, and, most endearingly, my friend.

JOHN DAVID (J. D.) WALT JR.
Dean of Asbury Theological Seminary Chapel
Pentecost 2005

The Quest for Effective Biblical Preaching

I suspect that people have been complaining since soon after the Day of Pentecost that preaching should be better than it is. The Apostle Paul confessed that the congregation at Corinth had made such complaints, and it sounds as if they had registered those complaints rather forcefully. "His letters are weighty and strong, but his bodily presence is weak, and his speech contemptible" (2 Corinthians 10:10). Nor had they made their judgment in a vacuum; they were comparing Paul's pulpit work with that of Apollos and Cephas, and one gets the feeling that Paul was coming out badly in Corinth's homiletical sweepstakes (1 Corinthians 1:10-17). I concur fully with Paul's argument that the major issue in preaching is the cross of Christ, and yet, if I know anything about human nature (and Paul was nothing if not human), I read some very human elements into his defense when he insists that his preaching was "not with eloquent wisdom," allowing us to infer that Apollos and some other preachers may have tended to outshine Paul in such matters.

In truth, Paul was fortunate in having to compete only with Cephas and Apollos at the preaching level, and a variety of philosophical lecturers in the secular marketplace of ideas. The twenty-first-century preacher has to pit talents and insights with radio, television, movies, and Internet — all of which pride themselves on being able to buy the best of talent, though one often wonders at the judgment demonstrated in their purchases. Paul could joust in the arena of ideas at Mars Hill, and if the occasion had presented itself, at learned academies in Alexandria and Jerusalem and Rome, but Paul's current successors speak to people who are surrounded by learned journals and editorial opinion pieces, even if they don't read them that often. More than that, our contemporary audiences are constantly distracted by that which is facile and superficial and momentarily engaging.

So what Paul had to deal with in congregations that thought they deserved better, we contemporary pulpiteers meet in multiples. And forgive me, my preaching colleagues, but in this whole discussion my sympathies tend to be on the side of the demanding congregations. Anyone who dares to expect an assembly of people, whether fifty or five hundred, to listen for whatever portions of an hour the sermon consumes is obligated to give something worthy of that accumulated collection of human time and life.

But how can we hope to command a hearing in a culture where so many voices of such variety and seductive skill are also laying claim to the attention of the people we hope to reach? The secret, quite simply (oversimply, some would say), is to use the resources that are *uniquely* ours. For one, that nearly indefinable gift we refer to as the anointing of the Holy Spirit. This power is singularly persuasive, even if we can't describe it or summon it at will. For another, the fact that we are appealing to a hunger more basic than the desire for gourmet food, sleek automobiles, and wonderfully diverting pleasures. If we have forgotten how basic is the need we're called and privileged to meet, we should remind ourselves how often the transitory commercial products try to package themselves in language that in truth belongs only to the eternal. And the eternal is our province. We're at home there, and others who use its language are poor if artful intruders.

But there is more, and it is that "more" that is the burden of what I want to say in this introduction. In addition to the anointing of the Spirit and in addition to that product-hunger we seek to meet, we have the Book. We are communicators who are blessed with a document like no other. We have the Bible. It is our privilege, our obligation, our inexhaustible resource. The people who come to hear a sermon can be gratified if the person in the pulpit moves comfortably in the waters of contemporary culture, with allusions that are knowledgeable and well-reasoned. But above all, they have a right to expect that this person who stands at what other generations called "the sacred desk" will know the Book. In each worship service we declare graphically that the Bible is our very special document. In liturgical churches the congregation sees the Bible carried in impressive processional along with the cross and perhaps some banners; in churches that eschew such ceremony the same point is made when the preacher holds the Book in hand while preaching, as evidence of authority for all that is said.

But the sermon that is preached may deny all the witness of the liturgy, whether it be the processional Bible or the extended gesture of the preacher. In some instances the Bible will be lost in a discussion of several theories as to the derivation of the text and cautious apologies as to its relevance to our day and time. In others the text will be greatly praised, then quite smothered by contemporary illustrations that are more likely to amuse or mystify than to enlighten. All too few unfold the Book in such a way that a congregation will feel its excitement, its authority, and its compelling relevance. And what is worse, since congregations so seldom hear such biblical preaching, in time they learn not to listen — or to listen for the superficial rather than the profound.

The author of the sermons in this book, Dr. Ben Witherington III, is a biblical scholar; but before he attained that academic rank, he was a parish pastor, and he has never lost his love for the parish. An old saying among the clergy defines a sermon as something a preacher will go halfway around the world to deliver but will not cross the street to hear. Not so with Ben. As a faculty colleague, I know I will see Ben as a worshipper in our seminary chapel services on Tuesdays and Thursdays. I know him as a faithful and involved member of a local congregation. On those occasions when I have preached with him in the congregation, I have found him to be an engaged worshipper. He does not simply listen to a sermon, he becomes part of it with the preacher. He believes in preaching, and the more biblically attractive the sermon, the more enthusiastically he supports it.

Does it matter that a preacher of the Word also be a glad listener to the Word? I believe it matters deeply. I suppose it's possible to be an artist who never visits a museum of art, or a writer who never reads poetry or novel or essay, or a preacher who doesn't care to listen to sermons, but if so, such individuals are rare. The preacher is first of all a believer, a worshipper, a God-adorer. Before delivering the Word, the preacher must be someone who hungers after the Word. In some of what the preacher hears, this hunger may be poorly satisfied, but even in the search for food we declare our belief in the divine order of eternal nourishment.

The sermons that follow are the work of someone who believes in preaching whether he is in the pulpit or in the pew, and I believe this quality shows through in each sermon. I'm not suggesting, of course, that these sermons will appeal to everyone, or that they will appeal in equal measure.

Some will find them shorter than in their tradition they are accustomed to hear. Fret not. As I advise the students in my homiletics classes, one doesn't need to tell all one knows in one sermon; the Lord willing, one will preach again. Besides, the content measure of a sermon is not how many words are spoken, but how many the people hear; and still more important, how many they retain.

Others, who cherish a verse-by-verse exposition of a biblical passage, will feel that these sermons are not as truly biblical as they should be. In most instances I would ask such persons to consider how much they know about the passage in question after hearing or reading a sermon; only then will they realize how much biblical content has been offered. In some cases, as in "Sincere — Sin's Here," the sermon is in truth almost a line-by-line exposition, without the lines being identified as "Now in verse three, etc."

Some will also argue that Dr. Witherington uses too many illustrations, and others will insist just as certainly that he uses too few. Personally, I will change my vote from side to side with particular sermons — although in truth, Ben uses more than I myself usually do. On the whole, the illustrative material is well-chosen; it's interesting, and it generally illuminates the point (which, after all, is what an illustration is supposed to do; if it doesn't illuminate the point, it's only a story, not an illustration). The illustrations come from a wide range of sources; they are obviously part of the person of the preacher, not something he scrounged up from some questionable collection.

Occasionally he falls into the preacher's trap of using a story that overwhelms the sermon. I think of "Them Dry Bones Gonna Rise," an Easter sunrise homily. The story from "a county in Ireland" that explains the origin of terms like "the wake," "dead ringer," "graveyard shift," and "saved by the bell" is very interesting. But the point of the sermon is quite lost in this collection of fascinating but only mildly-edifying information. Indeed, on the whole the potential of this sermon is obscured by a good deal of material that seems to be included only to maintain the interest of the audience, as if the preacher feared that at a sunrise service, attention were going to be difficult to maintain — as indeed, often it is. I would have been glad if the body of the sermon had spoken with the same commanding authority as the concluding paragraph.

There will also be mixed responses to Dr. Witherington's use of humor. This is to be expected. In humor, what is clever to one person is corny to another. Ben's humor is almost always clearly related to the text, rather than a joke that is dragged in by its scruffy neck. I would have been glad if he had relied more often on the innate humor in some of the biblical stories. Biblical characters so often plead with us to smile with them, and sometimes even to laugh out loud, while we insist on seeing them with painful solemnity. In doing so, we diminish their ability to speak to us as their kin.

One of the most persuasive and exemplary elements in these sermons is the use of titles. I confess readily that I speak from prejudice, because I believe deeply in the value of a good title. By a good title, I mean, first of all, that it be a title that encapsulates what the sermon is about. Such a title not only makes it easier for hearers to grasp and remember the sermon, it helps the preacher to remember what he or she has declared in shorthand to be the theme. A good title is also memorable. When the title is memorable, the odds are better that the sermon, too, will be remembered. And a good title is often appealing, so that seeing it in a newspaper advertisement, or on the church bulletin board, or in the Order of Worship, one is intrigued to see what the preacher will have to say.

Ben does this remarkably well. Sometimes it is simply the moving cadence of a great phrase, as in "The Mystery Made Manifest" or "The Glory of the Lord." In other instances he will set a popular phrase on its ear, as in "What in Creation?" or "We Haven't Got a Prayer," or "Excuse Me!" Some, like "Wise Men Still Seek Him," we've heard before, but they deserve repeating. His love of literature shows when he takes a magnificent phrase, like "Death Be Not Proud," or in a re-casting, "Love's Labor's Won." In "Fool's Goal," he works a pun, and also in "Sincere — Sin's Here." "The Temptations of God" has something of the ring of "what's going on here" that the late Harry Emerson Fosdick sometimes used so powerfully in his sermon titles. There's a danger, of course, in the pursuit of strong sermon titles, because sometimes the preacher can forget the text and the purpose of the sermon in his or her fascination with the title. I was troubled by this issue only in the sermon "Death Be Not Proud," when it seemed to me that the text was crowded out by the title.

I feel the church is desperately in need of strong, persuasive, biblical preaching. But I feel she needs just as much to hear clear doctrinal preaching. Studies of every kind indicate that our culture as a whole is vague in its knowledge of Christianity, even though a vast percentage of Americans identify themselves as Christians; and that even those persons who are closely tied to the church are surprisingly uncertain as to the "faith once delivered to the saints." This bodes ill not simply for the church, but for society as a whole and for individual souls. We are not likely to be much better than what we believe, and people who believe vaguely will live vaguely, with no certain, compelling sense of worth or direction.

So it is that in reading these sermons, I have been impressed at how naturally — indeed, almost subtly — good biblical preaching can become effective doctrinal preaching. Thus the two great needs of the contemporary Christian community are met at one and the same time; and we are reminded again that the source of Christian doctrine is in the Scriptures. None of these sermons is designated as a doctrinal statement, but I suppose that at least a third of them deal with doctrinal positions of the Christian faith — and that they do so without embarrassment or uncertainty.

Above all, these sermons remind us that nothing is more exciting than a biblical text that is visited with a clear mind and a warm heart. What could be more exciting than a God who stoops to conquer ("The Glory of the Lord")? Living as we do in a culture where power generally flaunts itself, what shall we say to a power — indeed, the Ultimate Power — that gladly diminishes itself? Or what will you say of a faith of such diverse, encompassing power that it can cause a woman to say as she dies from abuse in a death camp, "No hate, no hate"; and that can then one day convert the guard who had brutalized the woman; and finally, can cause the sister of the martyred woman to be able to forgive the man who had so inhumanely brought her sister to death ("To Err Is Human, to Forgive . . .")? Is there a plot anywhere in literature to compare with the Scriptures that introduce us to such a vast, encompassing faith?

And is there anywhere a description of us human creatures that is at the same moment more ennobling and more inescapably earthy than Paul's reminder that "we have this treasure in clay jars" (2 Corinthians 4:7)? With such a confidence the apostle could scorn the way his "outer nature [was] wasting away," because he knew his "inner nature [was] being renewed day by day" (4:16) ("Eternal Treasure in Earthen Vessels"). And as skilled as are some of our best playwrights and novelists in portraying sin and the lostness that comes from it, we have a feeling they all got their training, directly or indirectly, from the author of Psalm 51 ("Sincere — Sin's Here").

Let it be said: There is no book like the book we call The Holy Bible. Those of us who teach or preach from it are blessed with a document that should make us the envy of all other conveyors of ideas, of drama, or of insights in living. How eternally embarrassing if we neglect it or handle it ineptly! Only the Book itself could envision the shame such workers will ultimately feel; and only the Book itself can describe the fulfillment we know when we handle this document with glad, holy, thoughtful care.

DR. J. ELLSWORTH KALAS
Dean, Beeson International Center
for Biblical Preaching and Church Leadership
Asbury Theological Seminary

ADVENT AND CHRISTMAS

The Light Dawns

The Mystery Made Manifest

Psalm 18:1-9; Mark 13:32

Lo, He Comes with Clouds Descending

There is an old vaudeville sketch in which one person after another runs on stage shouting, "He's coming!" Finally, after this goes on for a while, one last person runs on stage and shouts, "He's here!" Everyone's curiosity and expectations have been aroused, but when the mysterious "he" finally appears it is someone rather ordinary who certainly does not live up to the way he has been introduced.

The first Sunday in Advent is when, interestingly enough, we contemplate not the First Coming of Christ, but rather the Second Coming. Charles Wesley's classic hymn "Lo, He Comes with Clouds Descending" was written quite specifically for this Sunday in the church calendar. What are your conceptions about the Second Coming of Christ? Do you wonder or think about such things very often at all? Whether you do or you don't, this Sunday at least gives the opportunity to reflect a bit about this often-foretold event.

Unfortunately, this event has been in our era the special focus for all sorts of theological weather forecasting, with some even going for the jackpot of predicting exactly when Christ will return. One thing, however, about the many such predictions that have occurred over the last two thousand years: they have all had a 100% failure rate. You would think this might stop such forecasting, but between the amnesia of the church about past failures and the kind of pious curiosity which, like God's mercies, seems to be new every morning, these predictions keep showing up everywhere from the *National Enquirer* to the sermons of reasonably sane ministers.

This is all rather amazing, not least because Jesus himself disavowed knowing the timing of this event. Mark 13:32, our New Testament text for this morning, is perfectly clear on this point: "Of that day or hour no one knows, not even the angels in heaven, not even the Son, only the Father." One would have thought that this pronouncement, which affirms that such knowledge is the possession only of God the Father, would have pre-empted such predictions. But no! It is interesting about this saying that it moves in a particular order from those who know least about this event and its timing, to those who know most — human beings, angels, the Son, the Father. We are on the low end of this chain of understanding, and it would be well if we remembered that.

I had to laugh a few years ago when a televangelist came on the TV and said that in his opinion Jesus would come back exactly two thousand years after he had first come. Now, this show was on in 1999 and the speculation about Y2K and all the hullabaloo about the turn of the millennium was in full swing, a hullabaloo that turned out to be much ado about nothing. Leaving aside the fact that the turn of the millennium technically occurred not at the end of 1999 but at the end of 2000, I had to laugh because this minister obviously didn't realize that Jesus was born somewhere between 8 and 2 B.C., with perhaps 4 to 2 B.C. being most likely.

In other words, if Jesus had been going to return exactly two thousand years later, he would have shown up well before this television show aired! Yet all this foolishness about date-setting should not be allowed to divert us from the importance of the promise about the fact of Christ's return, about which the New Testament is repeatedly emphatic. The timing of the Blessed Hope has never been and should never be an article of Christian faith, but the fact of it has always been such an essential belief. As the Apostles' Creed says, "From thence he shall come to judge the quick and the dead." But can we really know anything much about the character of that event, other than affirming it will happen, without engaging in pointless and idle speculation? Yes, I think we can — if we will focus on our Old Testament text for today in Psalm 18. But before we do that, let us consider a true story that reminds us afresh how *not* to approach this issue.

In 1969 or thereabouts I was riding on the Blue Ridge Parkway with a high school chum in my father's classic Chevy Bel Air (two tone, column shift, built like a tank). All of a sudden the clutch blew out, and, as the Bible says, "my countenance fell" because there are no gas or auto repair stations on the parkway. We ended up pushing the car down an exit ramp into a Texaco station with the help of another car, but the man who ran that station was as befuddled as we were about what needed to be done to fix the car. Being young lads, we decided to just park the car at the station off to the side, and hitchhike back to the center of the state from the mountains. We would worry about the rest once we got home. We were immediately picked up by a very elderly couple in an old black Plymouth, and we could not have realized the surprise we were in for. As it turns out, these folks were what mountain people called "flatlanders," by which is meant those who believe the world is flat rather than round.

My traveling companion and friend Doug (now a lawyer in Greensboro, North Carolina) could not believe what he was hearing, and, showing his disposition toward his future calling, he began to argue. I kept telling him to hush as we needed the ride. Back then, he obviously didn't recognize invincible ignorance when he saw it. He kept pressing the question: "Why do you believe the world is flat? Didn't you see the pictures from the NASA space orbits and trip to the moon by Neil Armstrong?"

The man who was driving dismissed that as all a Hollywood publicity stunt, but then finally got around to explaining the main reason he believed the world was flat. He said, "It says in the book of Revelations (and you need to beware of any sentence that begins that way and calls the last book of the Bible the book of Revelation*s* — plural) that the angels will stand on the four corners of the earth when Christ returns. The world couldn't be round if it has four corners, could it?" Of course, this man did not realize that the verse in question, Revelation 7:1, was not intended to teach cosmology so much as theology. The point was that God's messengers would come from all points on the compass to enact God's will. The problem with this man's interpretation was not that he took the text seriously, but that he took figurative apocalyptic language literally. If this is how *not* to approach the issue of the Second Coming, how should we approach it?

Theophany in the Offing

Have you ever wondered what it would actually be like to see God in person? Of course, in one sense this is a vain desire, for God the First Person of the Trinity is spirit, and does not have a body. The Old Testament is quite clear that no one has seen God, or at least no one has seen God's face and lived. Meeting your Maker face to face is depicted as being rather like picking up a thousand-volt electrical wire in a rain storm — a shocking, indeed deadly experience. This is in part why Jesus' claim is so shocking when he says in the Fourth Gospel, "Whoever has seen me has seen the Father." Only in Jesus is the Father visible in human form. Otherwise we only see the effects of the divine presence.

Most of us are accustomed to thinking of God working in nice, quiet, behind-the-scenes kinds of ways, or else through ordinary human means and methods. Our image of the work of God has become so domesticated that even Christians have come to see miracles as something of a surprise "intervention" into the natural order. Yet the Bible in numerous places makes evident that when God sets out to do something, there are signs and wonders, messages and messengers, miracles and mighty works. God even uses nature to reveal his anger or love, or as a tool to help someone. This last idea is part of what Psalm 18 is all about.

The word *theophany* comes from two Greek words meaning *God appearing*. We might say that when God responds to the psalmist's cry and comes down to aid the suppliant, "all earth breaks loose" — the mountains are shaken to their very foundations. The psalmist then imaginatively depicts God as rather like a flying, fire-breathing dragon with smoke coming out of his nostrils. We are told that God came through the clouds in his throne chariot and rode with the help of the angels to the psalmist's rescue, soaring on the winds. His voice is said to be like thunder (a popular idea in that age), his weapons were lightning bolts, and when he breathed the waters of the sea parted and were blown back, revealing the bottom of the ocean. This is Hebrew poetry, but the point is clear — when God comes down in person, look out, all heaven is breaking loose and it will be an earth-shattering, world-changing event.

Of course, this is highly metaphorical, but at the same time it is referential, and it is meant to make clear that God does come to the rescue, does reveal the divine presence to us and help us in our hour of need. He may even use the natural elements to accomplish such a purpose as he did in the Sinai to help his people escape across the Red Sea. Indeed, the psalmist seems to have that paradigmatic event in the back of his mind. It is interesting how the psalmist reacts to this radical rescue recounted in the psalm.

6

Reflections on and Response to God's Appearing

Such an encounter left our psalmist with two distinct impressions. The first is that he was given a glimpse into God's character, and the second is that it gave him a profound sense of gratitude. The latter is clear from the beginning of the psalm — "O Lord, I truly love you" — which is said in grateful response to the fact that God had rescued or saved the psalmist from a calamity. The God the psalmist believes in is a God of tremendous power who can intervene and rescue and also protect his people. Thus the psalmist says that God is his fortress (God protects him), his rock (God is solid and unchanging). God is like a shield as well when one is under attack from the various slings and arrows of outrageous fortune. Then God is called "the horn of my salvation," which seems to allude to the horns on the altar which one could flee to and grasp and so be deemed inviolate and safe, having reached "home base," so to speak. The psalmist says he was a drowning man and God came down and extracted him from the sea of his troubles, preventing him from dying. As the saying goes, the psalmist is telling us he was in deep waters, indeed, troubled waters.

The God who is depicted here is both a God of love and of great power, a God of compassion and at the same time a God of justice who intervenes on behalf of the oppressed. Reinhold Niebuhr, the great theologian, put it this way: "Love without power simply surrenders the world to power without love. How to make power express love, and love humanize power, is the distinctive task of the church for the next hundred years." When we follow the example of God and use our power to express love and our love to humanize power — for example, when we have taken part in building Habitat for Humanity houses for the poor — we will be emulating God.

One is struck by the stalwart trust the psalmist has in God, believing in God's ability to be trusted and to be trustworthy no matter how grave the situation. Too often we tend to panic and fear the worst instead of believing that God will respond to our cries. We are rather like the frantic and fearful lady on the ocean liner who came to the captain of the ship and asked: "Do ships like this sink very often?" "No, madam," came the reply. "Only once." We need the same steadfastness of faith in a God who will in the end set things right as the person who scrawled on the wall under Cologne Cathedral where he was hiding during World War II, "I believe in the dawn even though it is dark; I believe in God, even though he be silent now."

Coming to a Theater Near You

God has a track record. The psalmist thought of the Exodus events and then believed that God had rescued him just as God had rescued his forebears. The New Testament writers looked back to the psalms and the descriptions of theophany and indicated that the Second Coming of Christ will be very much like those descriptions. Jesus himself says in Mark 14:62 that we will see the Son of Man coming on the clouds with great power and in glory. It is not the timing of the event that matters, but that God has a track record, and what Christ promised, he will indeed one day perform, for he has both the love and the power to accomplish his aims for the good of humankind.

And so on the cusp of the Christmas season we remember that God has come many times to us, indeed that God has already come in Christ, and that he has promised to come again in Christ. It is not what we do not know about that future coming that should determine our faith or lack of it, but what we do know. And what we do know is that God has been rescuing the perishing by all kinds of means for all sorts of generations. It is not hard to believe that one day he will bring all those missions to a climax and a conclusion. The question for us is, *Where will we be going, and what will the Master find us doing, when he returns once more for a final time?*

Amen

The River of Life

Revelation 22:1-5; Ezekiel 47:1-12

Science Says

In an issue of *Christianity Today,* there was an interview with a non-Christian who is a scientist. His name, Robert Jastrow, is a household word in the scientific community. Inevitably, the conversation drifted to the matter of the origins of the universe. Prof. Jastrow pointed out that so far as he could see, the Big Bang theory, the theory that the universe began all at once, with a bang, seemed far and away the most probable explanation for the existence of the universe. When asked, however, how or what brought this about, Jastrow could only say that at present he did not know. He did not have enough data to even begin to theorize an answer. Jastrow is an agnostic. Pressed on the matter, he was asked if there was something he feared he might find in the search for the truth about our origins. He replied, "For the scientist who has lived by his faith in the power of reason, the story ends like a bad dream. He has scaled the mountains of ignorance; he is about to conquer the highest peak; as he pulls himself over the final rock, he is greeted by a band of theologians who have been sitting there for centuries."[1]

Scientists agree that God is outside the realm of scientific investigation. That leaves God the Creator out of any scientific theory about the origin of the universe. Even the scientist who is a Christian can only state his or her belief in God the Creator; he or she cannot espouse it in the scien-

1. Robert Jastrow, *God and the Astronomers* (New York: Norton, 1978), p. 116.

9

tific community, because God is not subject to scientific investigation. Thus, the scientists will continue to push back the moment of creation, to understand the origins of the universe, to try to discover how it happened. But they will not state that God the Creator is behind it all.

The Late Word from God

But if you asked Ezekiel what the source of all life was, he would have a clear answer. In Ezekiel 47 he gives us that answer in his marvelous depiction of the River of Life that flows forth from the temple of God. By depicting the River of Life flowing forth he was making a clear statement about life's origins. The temple is, of course, the residence of God, the place where his presence is found in a special way. Ezekiel is saying to the Israelites, "Only if God's presence is in our midst will there be life in us and among us and for us." This is also true of the church. If God is in the midst and at the center of what is done in a church, then there will be life in it. It will be anything but dull; in fact, it will be the most exciting thing one has ever experienced.

People, it seems, have a natural curiosity about origins. Scientists try to understand how the universe came into existence even if they can't admit that God is behind it. Archaeologists dig into the past to understand lost cultures, lost civilizations. Genealogists dig into the past to find out about the origins of their own families. (This can backfire. Mark Twain once said, "I paid a man $50 to research my family background, and $100 to cover it up again!")

But the answer to the question about the true origins and source of life is not to be found in rocks, or ruins, or in records and documents. God and God alone is the source of all existence, the Creator of the universe and of all people.

The Author and Fulfiller of Life

Yet God is not just the maker of life, an expert craftsman. He is also the one who invests life with its worthwhile qualities. God not only created human beings; he made them in his image. He bestowed his own life into us. There is a big difference between mere existence and real living. Almost all of us long to really live, not merely to exist.

Psychiatrists report that most patients nowadays arrive in their consulting rooms not with raw pain, but with a severe case of emptiness: "Doctor," they say, "I just don't feel anything. Something is missing and I don't know what it is. There must be more to life than this."

When a person loses the desire to truly live, lost also is the desire to be truly human. We all look for things or ways to help us really live — something to fill up the "God-shaped vacuum in the human soul," as Pascal put it. Yet the truth of the matter is that nothing can satisfy your longing for real life but God. Only he can give you life, with zest, life that is best, life that goes on forever. Now, you can try to fill up the longing in your soul for life by buying more, socializing more, working more, learning more, or even giving more. But to the extent that any of these efforts are only attempts to fill God's place in your life with something less than God, to that extent they are doomed to failure. Sam Levinson once said, "I set out in life to find the pot of gold at the end of the rainbow. Now I'm eighty and all I've got is the pot!"

A fulfilled life is one in which you use your talents to the fullest and give God the glory. God is at the center of all you do. Those who try to live their life without God are usually bored and restless searchers. Those who have God and don't use their talents in his service, for God's sake, can also feel unfulfilled. Faith without works is dead. But if God is with us and for us, and we work with him, then we can find peace and satisfaction in this life.

Geoffrey Studdert Kennedy, an Anglican priest, said, "I want to live, live out my life, not wobble through and then into the dark." The writer Jack London was right when he said, "I'd rather be ashes than dust. I'd rather my spark burn out in a brilliant blaze than be stippled by dry rot. I'd rather be a superb meteor than a sleepy planet. The proper function of man is to live, not exist."

The Search for Life

But once you recognize the true source of your life, once you begin to drink from the streams of everlasting waters, you begin to see that this life you have was not something you earned or deserved. Rather, it is a sacred and holy gift from God. Just as you would not abuse a gift the President of the United States gave you, so also you must not abuse or reject the gift of life that God gives you. The worst tragedy of all is that of the person who realizes at the end of his or her life that he or she has not truly lived, that his or her life has not been used wisely. Such was the case with a young soldier the writer Boris Pasternak described in *Dr. Zhivago:* facing execution, he was being dragged by guards to the edge of a cliff. Suddenly he broke out of his captors' grasp and fell to the ground and pleaded, "Forgive me, comrades. I did not mean it. It won't happen again. Don't kill me. I have not lived yet." Many of us have said that even to God: "Don't take me now. I have not lived yet."

There are also those who take life for granted and do not thank God for it. There are those who try to shape life into the image they have of it, to make themselves a comfortable world, as if the only point in life was creature comfort. There are those who would rather live with their illusion of what the world is all about rather than face the Creator God.

There is a story about Joan Rivers, the comedian. She had been fitted for contact lenses. The first night she used them while performing, she saw the audience clearly for the first time in years. It was so frightening to her that she excused herself and took off her contacts and returned onstage to entertain a more familiar, faceless blur. That's not unlike many of us spiritually. Our image of ourselves and others, as well as the magnificent beauty around us, is a dull blur, and often we would rather keep it that way. Yet we need to squarely face the fact that God created this universe, and us in his image, and because of that he expects more from us.

But there is another search going on — the search for the answer to life's problems. We look hopefully for ways to improve life and its flaws. Some of these efforts are monumental. Such is the story with the discovery of insulin. There was a world-renowned scientist who had a large laboratory with many young scientists working under him. Two of these young scientists received permission from their boss to pursue a treatment for diabetes, but he did not think the line of research they were taking would amount to anything. While the great man was off to England, the two young men discovered insulin and headlines went around the world. The headlines read: "Great scientist's lab discovered a new wonder drug for diabetes." The great man was interviewed in London and took credit for the discovery, although he had nothing personally to do with it. However, one reporter decided to go to the lab and find out more. Eventually he discovered who really made the great discovery, and asked them how it made them feel that their mentor got all the credit. One of them replied, "It doesn't matter who gets the credit, as long as a person gets the cure."

The Quick and the Dead

But there is also a danger in assuming that we can solve all our own problems, without God's help, with a bit more information. In the first twenty years of an American kid's life, he or she will see something approaching one million television commercials at the rate of a thousand a week. This makes the TV commercial the most voluminous information source in the education of American youth. Commercials teach a child three things. The first is that all problems are resolvable. The second is that all problems are resolvable fast. And the third is that all problems are resolvable fast through the agency of some product. It may be a drug. It may be a detergent. It may be an airplane or some piece of machinery, like a computer. The essential message is that the problems that beset people, whether it is lack of self-confidence or boredom or even money problems, are solvable by the inventions of modern-day technology.

Our text for today suggests quite another solution. It suggests that it will be God and the life that flows forth from him that will ultimately overcome the problems that plague all of us: disease, decay, death. When Ezekiel went outside the temple area he saw an ever-widening river flowing south and everywhere it went new life sprang up where life had never existed before. So deep and vast was this river that Ezekiel could not cross it. This is saying to us loud and clear that the depths of God's resources of life are unfathomable and unending. God never runs out of life or ways to help life.

Ezekiel saw a raging torrent that was so powerful that it overcame and overwhelmed the salty waters of the Dead Sea and brought life where it had never existed before. It brought health-giving trees. It brought meaningful human endeavor, meaningful work, where there had been no work before. Our God loves us so much that he desires us to have life and have it more abundantly. And he is willing to provide us with all that is necessary. Not just things for mere human existence, but for real spiritual life and health.

In the classic film *E.T. — the Extra Terrestrial* there is a poignant scene in which E.T. stretches out his finger and touches a dead flower and it blooms once more. So also with God: everything he touches turns to good (not to gold, despite the wishes of Midas and many others like him). And this good will go on forever, says Ezekiel. "Their leaves will not wither nor their fruit fall, but they will bear fresh fruit every month, because the water for them flows from the sanctuary."

Picture a world without waste, without want, without pollution, without disease, without death. It is what God offers us in the life to come if we will turn to him. It is what God will provide for us in full in the future when he concludes history and brings in his kingdom. And because God is with us, we can know this is true, like E.T., who said to Elliott, the boy who befriended him, pointing to his mind: "I'll be right here." God is already right here and the river of life is flowing from God to you.

So drink deeply from its stream. And dream God-given dreams. He offers life, to overcome strife. And his offer is just what it seems.

Jesus said to the Samaritan woman, "Everyone who drinks of ordinary water will thirst again. But whosoever drinks of the water that I shall give, will never thirst. The water that I shall give will become a spring of water welling up to eternal life." The woman said to him, "Sir, give me this water, that I may not thirst again."

Amen

The Glory of the Lord

Psalm 24:7-10; Luke 2:8-20; Philippians 2:5-11

The Glory of the Messiah

Without question, George Frideric Handel's *Messiah* is one of the most glorious musical compositions of all time. Few, however, seem to know the story of its origins.

Handel had wanted to be a writer of opera, and for a time he did well in Italy, until the market for new operas bottomed out and Handel found himself living hand-to-mouth. Handel moved to London, where he took to writing oratorios, which on the whole was not much more effective at keeping him gainfully employed. At the point of both poverty and despair, he was handed a remarkable libretto which focused on Isaiah and other Old Testament prophetic texts, as well as some New Testament ones. Handel's pulse quickened and his pen was sharpened and he began to write. He instructed the landlady of the building of flats where he lived to leave him alone until he had completed his work.

For many hours and some days in a row Handel did almost nothing but write music, barely even stopping to eat. When he was finally done and emerged from his study, he was heard to say, "I did think I saw the heavens open and the very glory of God indeed appeared to me." Listening to this glorious music, so very full of joy, it is easy to believe him. Something remarkable had happened to Handel. (John Wesley heard an early performance of this work and opined that "it might have a future"! What a prophet he was!)

But this entire story raises the questions, *What is glory?* and *What*

15

does it mean to see God's glory? Furthermore, how is that we can glorify God, and why should we do so, since presumably we can hardly add any luster to such an inherently glorious being. These are questions worth pondering at some length.

The Weight of Glory

Glory is an interesting concept. The Hebrew word for glory is *kabod,* which actually has as its root meaning *weightiness, heaviness, significance.* Thus Psalm 24, our psalm for today, asks the question "Who is this weighty king?" or, as our children might say, "Who is this heavy dude?" That, indeed, is the question posed as "Who is this king of glory?" in this psalm. Who is this significant Other who impinges upon our defenses and demands entrance into our inner sanctums? The answer is clearly given: it is the biblical God who is the King of Glory and who demands entry into us and our communities.

In due course the concept of glory came to be associated with the idea of the bright and shining presence that was perceived when God manifested himself to human beings. It came to be called the *Shekinah,* and it was said to radiate from the Ark of the Covenant, the sacred chest once depicted in that memorable movie *Raiders of the Lost Ark.* The Greek word for glory is *doxa,* and it, too, can have the meaning of a splendid or shining appearance; but the concept was also used to speak of giving glory (that is, praise and honor) to someone worthy of it. Hence we have the word *doxology* for a song or liturgy giving glory or praise to God.

It is striking how different all this is to some modern notions of glory. Much that is associated with glory in our day has to do with human achievement — things that we achieve, or do, or take. Glory is seen as something to be grasped with both hands because we only go around once in life. We must grab for all the gusto (and glory) we can get. Our world is filled with glory-grabbers rather than glory-givers, those who seek to grab movie headlines, carve out financial empires, or proclaim themselves the greatest athlete in their sport. We know all too well our world's definition of glory — seeing something you want and going out and taking it or winning it. Somehow there is a disconnect between these human conceptions of glory, and what the Bible is talking about.

Humbling Oneself, Giving Up Glory

It is striking that in the hymn we find in Philippians 2:5-11 we are in essence told that when it came to Jesus, giving and giving up were what amounted to glory for him. Paul puts it this way: "Though being equal to God, he did not take advantage of that, but rather stripped himself and took on the form of a human being, and a servant amongst human beings." Apparently for Jesus, stepping down and serving others rather than stepping up and being self-serving was the essence of glory. And notice God's response to Jesus' sacrifices: "Therefore God has highly exalted him and given him the name which is above all names." Here we have a divine King who stooped to conquer. George MacDonald, the Scottish writer, put it this way: "We were all looking for a King to slay our foes and lift us high; thou cam'st a little baby thing that made a woman cry." The glory of the Christ child came from who he was, what he gave up, and of course what he gave to others.

You see, the world has not only a skewed sense of glory, but a skewed sense of greatness. When we say the word *humility*, from the Latin *humilitas*, the image often conjured up is that of a person of low self-esteem or with an inferiority complex. The meek who Jesus says will inherit the earth one day are assumed to be the weak. I like the *Far Side* cartoon which shows a meek and mild-mannered, bespectacled man sitting across the desk from his accountant and looking worried. The caption says, "The day after the meek inherit the earth." The accountant is saying to the trembling man, "What you have here is a quite serious capital gains problem."

I am struck by the fact that the Bible never speaks of having humble feelings. Humility in the Bible has little or nothing to do with one's attitude or feeling about one's self. It certainly has nothing to do with feelings of low self-worth. Consider the exemplar — Christ. If there was one man who walked this earth who did not have feelings of low self-worth or an inferiority complex it was surely Jesus. Humility in his life and in the New Testament in general is an action word — it refers to the action of a strong person deliberately stepping down and serving others. Jesus chose to be the servant of all and he showed that the path of glory is the path of giving up, sacrificing for others, serving; the path of glory is not paved with feelings of low self-worth. Our Pauline text for today suggests that glory is not as advertised by the world. Indeed, this text suggests that glory has to do with emulating Christ's "career path" of self-sacrificial service. It begins, "Have this mind in yourself that was also in Christ Jesus." We learn from this text that real glory comes from setting aside the façade of self-importance and instead having the mindset that was in Jesus. What a different concept of glory that entails. And this brings us to our Gospel text for today — all about the shepherds.

"They Glorified God"

According to Luke, the first ones on the scene other than the Holy Family when Jesus was born were shepherds. And to listen to Luke's tale they had quite a remarkable night. First angels appeared to them while they were minding their business tending their flocks. These angels announced the birth of Jesus, but the text also stresses that as they did so they were glorifying God, saying that the highest glory or praise should be given to God for sending the Savior. Now if even angels, certainly more glorious and supernatural beings than humans, are busy giving glory rather than glorifying themselves, this should certainly give us a clue about the problematic nature of humans glorifying themselves.

Shepherds were often looked down upon because of their trade, not least because it involved contact with animal corpses and their hides, which made them ritually unclean, at least for a time. The word *glory* and the word *shepherd* would not have been readily associated with one another in the minds of ancient Jews. Perhaps that is why God chose them to receive the most glorious announcement first. It was not about them being worthy or glorious; it was about them giving glory to the glorious One who had come. Paradoxically, in their humble station and attitude they more resembled the Christ both in his birth and in his later, chosen *modus operandi* than did King Herod, who lived in nearby Jerusalem and sought to glorify himself forever through the enormous building projects he commissioned — the Temple, the Herodium, Caesarea Maritima, and many others.

Notice how at the end of the story it is these very shepherds who go forth from seeing Jesus in very humble circumstances and yet, apparently because of the correspondence between the angelic announcement and the reality they witnessed, they went forth from the manger glorifying God and announcing Christ's coming in such remarkable fashion that we are told that, "Everyone marveled at all the shepherds told them." The shepherds became the first human proclaimers of the gospel, a fact which should humble any minister then or now — for it wasn't about credentials or ability; it was about witnessing and willingness and availability.

In God's economy of things, then, glory appears in strange places and involves unexpected persons. I must leave you with a story. I was working in the mountains of North Carolina, near Burnsville, with the rural poor of Appalachia one spring break, and it was my duty to pick up children and bring them to an Easter egg hunt and picnic. There was one family, well back up in the hills, who had a five-year-old son named Carl, who had never set eyes on anyone other than his own family. I spent a long time trying to convince the mother to let me take Carl to the party. She finally relented and told me she would have him ready at 6 a.m., which was when I needed to collect him since there were many others I had to pick up as well in my pickup truck.

The light was dawning over the mountain when I arrived at Carl's small clapboard house, and there he was, his face scrubbed raw, with his only decent clothes on, sitting on the front porch waiting for me. Now, Carl had one possession of note, and only one — his very own goose. And so it was not entirely a surprise when I saw him holding a great big goose egg. When I got out of the truck and came over to pick him up he handed me the egg and said, "Here, Mr. Ben, this is for the children who ain't got any Easter eggs." Had Carl been looking closely, he would have seen me beginning to weep, for in that moment I had seen the glory of God (as the Gospel of John says, "We have seen his glory"), which involves self-sacrificial love. If even shepherds and poor children like Carl can honor and glorify God in that way surely we can as well — especially at this season of the year. Carl's gift reminded me of the Christmas hymn that says,

> What can I give him, poor as I am?
> If I were a shepherd, I would bring a lamb.
> If I were a wise man, I would do my part.
> Yet what I can I give him,
> Give him my heart.

There is no more glorious thing you could give on this night, nor a better way to glorify God, than to give yourself to Christ who awaits you in the manger with open arms.

Amen

19

Logos Logic

John 1:1-18

Trailing Clouds of Glory

Tallulah Bankhead was undoubtedly one of the most flamboyant and color-
ful women of her era. She talked loud; she dressed loud; she was not known
for her subtlety. She was also not much given to attending church. But on
one occasion she heard that there was to be some real pageantry and ceremony at the local Catholic cathedral, for a famous bishop was coming to
town for a special worship service. She decided she wanted to go and see
what would happen. Characteristically, she got there early so she could have
the seat of her choosing (realizing, I suppose, that "many are called but
pews are chosen") and she positioned herself right on the aisle in the second
row so she could look down the aisle and see the whole procession.

The service began promptly. The organ cranked up, and then the ac-
olytes and the crucifer started down the aisle, followed by the choir, the
priests of that particular diocese, and finally the bishop himself. The
bishop was decked out in a shimmering gold robe, and he had chosen to
perform the role of carrying the censer himself. As he began to proceed
down the aisle he was swinging the censer mightily to the rhythm of the
music, and the clouds of incense were going up. (Indeed, one could say
that the whole congregation was getting incensed so permeating was the
smell.) Finally the bishop reached the spot where Tallulah was positioned,
standing along with the rest of the congregation for the procession, and instinctively she reached out and tugged on the bishop's robe as he went by
and said, "Darling, your gown is divine, but your purse is on fire."

The Son of God, unlike the bishop, did not enter the world trailing clouds of glory, nor was there a great congregation standing at attention when he came. As we learn every Christmas, Jesus came into the world in a humble manner and by humble means — a feeding trough in the back of some relative's house, in all probability. It has been said that he came this way to make clear that no one and no condition of life was beneath his dignity. He stooped to conquer; he condescended so we might be lifted up.

But lest we think that Jesus only came from Bethlehem into this world, the prologue to the Gospel of John suggests a much longer journey from a place much farther away, a journey set in motion from before the foundation of the world. The first paragraph of John's Gospel is actually part of a hymn, or at least hymnic prose, and it tells the story of the Word. We are meant to hear echoes of the beginning of Genesis — "In the beginning God created the heavens and the earth." How did he do it? By speaking a word into the void. Our Evangelist is telling us that God's work of creation had a sequel which was without equal — the work of redemption.

Word Up, about the Word That Came Down

It was C. S. Lewis who said that when the author of the play walks on the stage, you know that the play is over, but in this case we are being told that the author of the whole human drama has come on the scene to fix and finish what we had marred and messed up. He is called here the Word, or, in Greek, the *Logos*. Our Evangelist believes that where a person has come from and how far they have come tells us a lot about that person, and indeed this is true. It is being suggested that we should in one sense judge a person by how far they have come in life, not how far they have gone. (Some people, after all, are described as being born on third base and thinking they hit a triple!)

But in the case of the *Logos* there could have been no one who came from farther away or longer ago, and no one who could have come farther to save you and me. The Evangelist says that the Word existed before the foundation of the universe — indeed the Word was co-creator of the universe, such that human creatures were all made in his image. It even goes so far as to equate the Word with God! We learn later in the hymn that it is the only-begotten Son of God who is called both the Word and God in this hymn, which means that there is more than one person in the Godhead.

This is, to say the least, heavy stuff. God in the end didn't just send another angelic or a merely human messenger, be it prophet, priest, or king. God "cared enough to send the very best" — God came in person, in the person of the only-begotten Son.

But why is he called the Word or *Logos* here? Because the author wants to make clear that if you are trying to figure out the mind, the wisdom, the logic, the sense of God you need to consider his only-begotten Son. He is God's plan for redemption come in the flesh. The Son of God may not be all we would like to know about God, but in terms of salvation it is all we need to know about God. God comes as Jesus, and we may trust that God is indeed like Jesus. If you want to figure out the character, nature, plan, hopes, dreams of God, you only need look at his Son — he's the spitting image of the Father.

Darkness at the Edge of Dawn

But this story is very much like a Rembrandt painting — there is darkness that surrounds and frames the piercingly bright light of the Word. Imagine a creator God who made creatures who rejected him. Nothing can be more tragic than when children repudiate their parents, but this is exactly what we are told was afoot in the human drama — "He came unto his own, but his own received him not." Jesus the Jew arrived in Judea saying, "Family, I am home!" and the locals received him not, indeed the so-called king of the Jews tried to kill him. He stood up in the synagogue in Nazareth, and his neighbors received him not. In John's Gospel we are even told that Jesus' brothers, befuddled and bewildered and envious of their brother (like the brothers in the story of Joseph), did not believe in him during his ministry (John 7:5). Jesus instead had to enlist the least, the last, and the lost as his disciples: IRS men and fishermen and revolutionaries, an odd gaggle of geese, and they often appear not as the Magnificent Twelve but as the Dirty Dozen, or better, as the *duh*-sciples. Jesus' kin and neighbors and Jewish relatives didn't exactly roll out the red carpet for him. His own disciples don't quite understand him.

In John's Gospel, the prologue is essential to understanding what follows, because unless you know where Jesus actually came from — which is to say, from God and as God — you are not going to understand Jesus. His story will sound more like a fractured fairy tale than the Gospel truth if you do not know the essential truth that Jesus is the incarnation of God. John puts it this way: "The Word took on flesh."

The pre-existent divine Son of God took on a human nature in the womb of Mary without ceasing to be the divine Son of God. That's a mouthful, and in theological terms it is called the Incarnation. The great English poet John Donne put it this way: "'Twas much when man was made like God long before/but that God should be made like man, much more."

The mind, the character, the nature, the plan of God was all revealed in this one person, Jesus. It's a staggering assertion. But that is God's logic and the logical solution to our dilemma. We sometimes think, as the British would say, that it is over-egging the pudding to say that this person or that person is the greatest who ever lived, but in this case there is no human rhetoric grand enough to encompass this truth. Jesus is hands-down the greatest person to have ever existed.

In John's Gospel, if you know that the Word came from God, as God, and returns to God, you know the whole arc of the story of the Son of God. The earthly ministry is just the middle act of the drama, and you all know how befuddling it can be to arrive at the theater in the middle of a play — how much more so in the middle of the story of our redemption!

Logos Logic

One of my college chums was Thomas V. Morris. We took religion and philosophy classes together at Carolina and he went on to become a famous philosopher, teaching at Notre Dame and winning national awards. He now spends his time speaking to Fortune 500 companies about the philosophy of business and success and lives at Wrightsville Beach, North Carolina. Lucky him!

While he was still at Notre Dame he wrote an important book entitled *The Logic of God Incarnate.* One of the profound things he says in this book is that God came not so that we could know he was real, or so that we could identify with God, though those things are true. No, the logic of God Incarnate involves more than just to know that God cared.

Rather, Jesus came to die for us. We needed more than just an answer to questions about whether God is real and whether he can relate to us. We needed a solution to the human dilemma. The dilemma may be summed up as follows: that we have all fallen and we can't get up. Jesus himself explains the logic of the *Logos* coming in person when he says, "The Son of Man did not come to be served but to serve, and to give his life as a ransom in place of the many." Jesus was the man born to die. It is a paradoxical logic, but nonetheless a logic that we cannot live without if the least, the last, and the lost are to become the first, the most, and the found.

In John's Gospel Jesus doesn't just *give* the resurrection; he *is* the resurrection. He doesn't just *offer* life; he *is* eternal life. He doesn't just *show* the way; he *is* the way — and when he says, "Before Abraham was, I am," he is claiming to have existed before the time of Abraham, indeed to have existed as God before all time. This is the savior who came to us in the person of Jesus. Could we possibly take in, comprehend, grasp anything this monumental, this stupendous?

We might well be led to feel like Charlie Brown in that *Peanuts* strip in which he, Lucy, and Linus are looking up at the clouds and describing what they see in the clouds. Linus speaks first and says, "I see Beethoven composing a piano sonata." Lucy says, "I see Van Gogh painting his famous *Starry Night* painting." She then turns to Charlie Brown and says, "What do you see, Charlie Brown?" He responds: "I was going to say I see a duck and a pony, but I think I'll just hush." Perhaps we feel a bit like Charlie Brown in the presence of this great wonder and mystery. It has been said that in the Gospel of John, Jesus strides across the stage of history like a God. It has also been said that this Gospel is shallow enough for a baby to wade in, but deep enough for an elephant to drown in. How true! Can we possibly understand the logic of this plan and this person, the divine Son of God?

The Last Word

Well, yes, in fact, we can. God boiled the whole salvation plan down into a one-man mission, sending his only-begotten Son to pull it off, and his Son sent the Holy Spirit so we could understand it, and be convicted, convinced, and converted. The prologue climaxes with these words: "And we beheld his glory, glory as of the only begotten of the Father. For the Law came through Moses, but grace and truth through Jesus Christ." If we unpack this a bit, we see that it is a short course in Johannine vocabulary — light in this poem refers to revelation, life means salvation, glory indicates the radiant presence of God, grace means God's undeserved favor, and hopefully truth speaks for itself. Certainly when Jesus came, Truth spoke for himself.

We are being told that it is "one-stop shopping" with Jesus — he is all the things we need wrapped up in one person to save the soul, renew the mind, give hope to the heart, heal the wounds of outrageous fortune, bind us together, create a more perfect union of believers, save the world. And best of all, we are being told that if the first disciples, who were often theologically challenged, could receive it, believe it, even begin to understand it — if they could see the radiant presence of God in the face of Jesus, so can we.

I must leave you with a final story. I was sitting in the lobby of Joseph-Beth Booksellers in Lexington the other day and there was a mother with her ever-so-inquisitive child trundling along beside her. The child kept asking his mother about hell. He asked, "Could I ever do something bad enough to go to hell?" His mother said, "I can't imagine a child doing something that bad." He kept pressing the issue. "Who would guard me and keep me from going there? You are my mommy, you wouldn't let me go there, would you? You would rescue me, right?" The young boy's mother, on the verge of both exasperation and tears, said, "Of course we would rescue you; your parents love you and would never allow you to go there." This seemed to satisfy him.

John's Gospel has a similar answer. It says that though we have in fact gone into the dark, though we have in fact loved darkness more than light, though we have lost our way, though we may feel we could never comprehend, never mind deserve, salvation, yet "God so loved the world that he gave his only begotten Son such that whosoever believes in him shall not perish, but have everlasting life." God came all the way down the stairsteps of heaven to rescue his lost and straying children. He came in the person of Jesus, he called us by name, he took us by the hand, and he will not lead us astray — and each one of us, each one of us has an opportunity to behold his glory, receive his grace, and know his truth. And that, indeed, is the logic of the *Logos*, the Word that came down and took on flesh.

Amen

For Study and Meditation

"The Mystery Made Manifest"
(Psalm 18:1-9; Mark 13:32)

- Meditate on Psalm 18:1-9.
  - Read the passage out loud.
  - Read the passage again, asking God to bring to the surface words or phrases he longs for you to hear.
  - Read the passage once more, speaking it as a prayer for yourself and for others. Focus specifically on verse one through six. Ask God to help you to see him in the everyday experiences of your life.
- Journal about a time when you have seen God appear in your own life.
- Write down the specifics of this event with as much detail as you can remember. Do not be surprised if God brings to mind new details and insights as you write. Feel free to paint or draw to express the details of this event if you wish.
- Confess your lack of trust in God's steadfastness and faithfulness. Ask God to give you the "stalwart trust" of the psalmist and the strength to wait expectantly for him.

THOUGHTS FOR FURTHER REFLECTION

"I love you, O Lord, my strength!"

Psalm 18:1

"It is not the timing of the event that matters, but that God has a track record, and what Christ promised, he will indeed one day perform, for he has both the love and the power to accomplish his aims for the good of humankind."

Ben Witherington III

"God, of your goodness, give me yourself, for you are sufficient for me. I cannot properly ask anything less, to be worthy of you. If I were to ask anything less I should always be in want. In you alone do I have all."

Julian of Norwich (1342-ca. 1416)

"People see God every day, they just don't recognize him!"

Pearl Bailey

"The River of Life"
(Revelation 22:1-5; Ezekiel 47:1-2)

- Worship God by giving him thanks for giving you this day to live. Sing or listen to a favorite hymn or praise song and offer a prayer of praise.
- Silence is a difficult spiritual discipline, but important for remaining centered in our busy lives. Spend at least fifteen minutes (more as you are able) in silence and reflection today.
- Fast from food or something else specific for half a day (more as you are able).
- More than any other discipline, fasting reveals to us what our source of life truly is. Ask God to reveal to you areas which you have yet to fully surrender to him. Journal or list the areas you still need to give to God. When you break your fast, celebrate! Thank God for being the source of all life. Ask him to give you courage to truly live your life for him.

Thoughts for Further Reflection

"There is a big difference between mere existence and real living."

Ben Witherington III

"A fulfilled life is one in which you use your talents to the fullest and give God the glory. God is at the center of all you do."

Ben Witherington III

"Be such a man and live such a life, that if every man were such as you, and every life a life like yours, this earth would be God's Paradise."

Phillips Brooks, American Episcopal Bishop

"Be not afraid of growing slowly; be afraid only of standing still."

Chinese Proverb

"Eternal God, my sovereign Lord, I acknowledge all I am, all I have is yours. Give me such a sense of your infinite goodness that I may return to you all possible love and obedience."

John Wesley

"The Glory of the Lord"
(Psalm 24:7-10; Luke 2:8-20; Philippians 2:5-11)

- Serve at an area soup kitchen or homeless shelter or volunteer at your local church. Make this a regular part of your week. Pray that God will help you to see that the way to true glory is "stepping down to step up."
- Pray through Philippians 2:5-11. Pray that God will empty you out in service to others. Pray that his glory would radiate through your life and flow through to others.
- Write a letter of gratitude to someone whose service to you (or others)

has blessed you. Thank them for their servant-heart and let them know what an impact they make on you and others. You might even offer to do something for them!

THOUGHTS FOR FURTHER REFLECTION

"The glory of the Christ child came from who he was, what he gave up, and of course, what he gave to others."

Ben Witherington III

"There is no more glorious thing you could give . . . nor a better way to glorify God than to give yourself to Christ who awaits you in the manger with open arms."

Ben Witherington III

"He who refreshes others will himself be refreshed."

Proverbs 11:25

"I beg you, O Lord, that the fiery and sweet strength of your love may absorb my soul away from all things that are under heaven, that I may die for love of your love as you deigned to die for love of my love."

St. Francis of Assisi (1181-1226)

"Holy Spirit, think through me 'til your ideas are my ideas."

Amy Carmichael (1867-1951)

"*Logos* Logic"
(John 1:1-18)

◆ Read John 1:1-18 aloud a few times slowly and prayerfully. Write down words or phrases that stand out to you.

- ◆ Journal on your reading(s) of John 1:1-18. Allow yourself to write and reflect freely. Use whatever form is best for you — writing, composing poetry or lyrics, drawing, painting — to express yourself.
- ◆ Memorize part or all of John 1:1-18 over the next few days. This is a wonderful passage to commit to memory and carry around with you. The words John wrote here so long ago will encourage you as you recall them, serving as a reminder of the personal nature of our God.

Thoughts for Further Reflection

"The Son of God may not be all we would like to know about God, but in terms of salvation it is all we need to know about God. God comes as Jesus, and we may trust that God is indeed like Jesus. If you want to figure out the character, nature, plans, hopes, dreams of God, you only need look at his Son — he's the spitting image of the Father."

Ben Witherington III

"Glory be to thee, O Lord, glory to thee, O Holy One, glory to thee, O King!"

John Chrysostom (347-407)

"The Word became flesh and blood and moved into the neighborhood. We saw the glory with our own eyes, the one-of-a-kind glory, like Father, like Son, generous inside and out, true from start to finish."

John 1:14, *The Message*

EPIPHANY

The Light Appears

Transfigured

Isaiah 6; Revelation 4

Isaiah's Vision

It happened to Isaiah a long time ago. He went into the temple and encountered more than he had counted on. He says, "I saw the Lord. . . ." The Israelites in Isaiah's day saw the temple in Jerusalem as the juncture between earth and heaven, and there the prophet had a close encounter with the Almighty. The thing about any such encounter, if it really is God one is encountering, is that it is a matter of communion between two beings of very different orders. A close encounter with God, paradoxically enough, both widens and narrows the gap between us and God. It *widens* it because any such genuine encounter makes clear that God is God and we are not! Notice what Isaiah says: "Woe unto me, I am a man of unclean lips." God is the Holy One, and Isaiah, even with his priestly and prophetic pedigree, is a mere mortal. Worship happens when the creature realizes that he or she is not the Creator, and bows down before and adores the one who is. That is true worship. It is about giving up, surrendering, presenting yourself as a living sacrifice, bowing down, recognizing and restoring the creation order of things.

But the gap is also *narrowed* in the sense that when we bow down, God condescends to come down to our level and honors our worship. Then we encounter God. Worship creates a communion that maintains the separation of God and humankind. G. K. Chesterton once said words to the following effect: "A creature is not made so that he can worship himself any more than you can fall in love with yourself — or if in a fit of narcissism you do so, it will be a monotonous courtship."

33

Worship is not about our cozying up to God, our buddy or pal. There is, of course, intimacy to be shared with our *Abba*, but we are in no way being set up in a partnership of equals in worship. A partnership or *koinonia* between equals results in fellowship, not worship. So let us be clear — the experience of Isaiah was worship. Any experience which seeks to put us up on God's level is not worship. It is inappropriate, even shocking familiarity — indeed, it can even be called idolatry. God condescends and remains God; we do not ascend and become as gods. If we once ceased to be the creature and became absorbed by the deity we would no longer be capable of worship. Worship inherently implies a distinction between the worshiper and the one worshiped. Furthermore, when real worship happens we become even more creaturely, even more of what we were intended to be as image of God. We become eternal worshipers of the Triune One.

The English word *worship* actually comes from the combination of two words, *weorth* and *scipe* from the Old English. It has to do with honoring or giving homage to one who is worthy to receive such praise, attention, obeisance: "Thou art worthy." We, by contrast, are not worthy of such absolute, unconditional devotion and adoration. Idolatry is the polar opposite of true worship. It is ascribing deity to, and serving and sublimating oneself before, something that is less than God Almighty: a human ruler, a parent, a friend, a conqueror, a lover, a teacher or mentor, or even oneself. There are many forms idolatry can take.

Ezekiel's Experience

But consider another Old Testament worship experience. Just like Isaiah, Ezekiel was taken by surprise by God, who just keeps coming our way in divine condescension, even in surprising places. Isaiah had his close encounter and was transfigured in the temple. But Ezekiel was sitting by the Kebar River in exile in Babylon, probably swatting mosquitoes the size of small birds, when God gave him the awesome vision of a throne and a chariot. Worship was not a matter of being in a holy place for Ezekiel. Rather, what he learned is that "the earth is the Lord's and the fullness thereof" — even the land of the Exile. God's presence can be encountered anywhere, at any time.

This vision is also crucial for John of Patmos, who sees a vision not unlike Ezekiel's. To be sure, John also was not in church or synagogue when he saw the *mysterium tremendum* recorded in Revelation 4. He, too, was in exile, on a rock pile off the coast of modern Turkey, when he received a vision while in the Spirit on the Lord's day. He was in the Spirit, not in the church. It's not a matter of holy space; it's a matter of holy, or at least receptive, condition. But the mention of the Lord's day may suggest a holy time, a time for worship. It is no accident that Ezekiel had his vision on the very day he should have been anointed priest in the temple in Jerusalem. It was a holy time for him.

Caught Up in the Spirit, Caught Up in Worship

Our proper text for today, Revelation 4, raises compelling questions about the nature of worship, and our posture and preparation for it. So often we will hear people say, "I don't go to that worship service because I don't get anything out of it." But wait a minute! Who is supposed to be doing the worshiping here? If it is the congregation, then the primary question should be, where can I go to best *give* praise and worship to God, not where can I go to *get* the most out of it.

There was an elderly woman in my home church who could barely see or hear. Yet there she was each Sunday, sitting near the front and participating in worship with vigor. One day a young woman asked her why she was there since she could not really hear much of what was being said or see much of what was happening. Her reply was memorable: "I am not here for what I can get out of the service but for what I can give. I get the bulletin mailed to me and I get out my magnifying glass and I read it through, and then read the Scriptures and the hymns we will sing. I think and pray through what may be God's Word for me in this. Thus when I come to the service I am ready to worship, and I give that to God, even though I am getting back perhaps less than some in that particular hour." The young woman was stunned. Caught up in the consumer mentality of many in our society, and applying it to worship, she had just assumed that one chose a worship service, or for that matter a church, on the basis of what one could get out of it, not on the basis of where God might be best pleased to receive our worship and service.

Worship is not, and never was intended to be, a spectator sport, or the performance of the few for the benefit of the many couch potatoes in the pew. The consumer approach to worship puts the emphasis almost entirely on the wrong syllable. It leads to pastors desperately seeking to change worship patterns so that worship services will attract bigger crowds, on the theory that worship should be a matter of giving the people what they want and crave. Wrong: worship is a matter of giving to God what he desires and requires of us. If you end up with a nice buzz because of it, that's a bonus and a by-product; it's not what we are striving for. John of Patmos was not looking for a more *au courant* worship service when he was in the Spirit on the Lord's day and received a vision.

Consider first what was the prerequisite for John receiving the vision. It was not that the right mood was being set by the music. It was not that he was in the right place. It was rather that he came prepared for an encounter in holy time; he came prepared to give honor and praise and glory on the Lord's Day. He was wide open to the Spirit to such a degree that the text says he was *in the Spirit*. Notice, it does not say that the Spirit was in him, though that was also true. No, he had already immersed himself in the divine presence before the vision came. This likely means that he had prepared his heart to worship, he had repented of his sins, he had been shriven or cleansed, and so he boldly approached the Presence and immersed himself in God.

And when God gave him the vision, what a vision it was! It was a vision of heavenly worship that transfixed and transfigured him. He saw representative samplings of all the different orders of creature lifting up God on God's throne: animals, humans, angels, all were symbolically present in the Presence of God, lifting up God on his throne. The twenty-four elders represented God's people, both old and new, and though they were given thrones, they fell down before him who was on the throne and worshiped him. The living creatures with eyes everywhere, seeing all there was to see, looked in wide-eyed amazement, and never stopped saying, "Holy, holy, holy, is the Lord God Almighty, now and forever!"

Worthwhile Worship

Why is God worthy of such worship? Because he is the Creator God who made all the creatures for just such a purpose. "It is the chief aim of humankind to love God and enjoy and adore him forever," is how the Heidelberg Catechism puts it. The most important act on earth is worship. It completes the intended life cycle of all creatures great and small. The chief end of humankind and human history is not the salvation of all persons. I will say that again. *Salvation is not the point and goal of human history.* It is but the means to the ultimate end, which is the proper worship of God by all creatures. It is, of course, true that were we to go on to Revelation 5 we would also learn that worship is intended to include and focus not only on the Creator God, but also the Redeemer God, namely the Lamb who is at the same time the Lion of the Tribe of Judah! But redemption is a means to the end of true worship, a worship in which every knee shall bow and every tongue confess.

So let's review what we have learned: First, true worship requires that we be in the Spirit at the appropriate time for worship (that is, the Lord's day). Second, this in turn implies that we come as true worshipers wide open to giving praise and glory to God, having already received the grace necessary to be able to do so, having put aside all distractions and the sin that so readily encumbers us. Only so are we prepared to receive what God will give: the proclamation of his truth and the comfort of his presence. Third, worship is chiefly what *we* do: we come to give honor and glory to the Worthy One. We come to give primarily, rather than to get. But hear the good news: God *also* comes to give! God bows down as we bow down to God. God comes to relate to, empower, heal, save, give vision to his people, and proclaim his truth. Fourth, the vision John received was of heavenly worship.

The chief aim of worship is that we be caught up in love, wonder, and praise of God, and in so doing get a glimpse of the heavenly worship that happens when and as we are worshiping. In other words, we get a glimpse of what is happening above, which is also a vision of our destiny: when heaven comes down, and glory fills our souls, and we become God's music, and we become God's true temple, and we become the bride, and we become the new Jerusalem that God's holy presence comes to inhabit for ever and ever. But that is a subject for a homily on another occasion. For now I leave you with a story.

At the end of a tour of two of the lands of the Bible in August of 2001, my intrepid group of pilgrims, who had been sojourning for two weeks in Greece and Italy, spent their last Sunday morning in the catacombs on the edge of the eternal city, Rome. We were some two hundred feet underground, and it had been arranged that we would worship in one of the niches where the saints had been buried for hundreds of years, though their caskets and coffins had long since been moved elsewhere. Only the holes in the walls, going up some twenty feet on either side of the narrow barrel-vaulted apse in which we stood, were visible. Yet there was a heavy sense that the saints were worshiping there with us, and we with them. I preached on 2 Corinthians 4, and we all took communion together. Our guide, Giorgio Abate, a nominal Catholic, had been deeply moved by the service, perhaps especially by the singing, and asked if he, too, might share in the communion. We, of course, were delighted he would ask. All of us, our hearts full of praise after a long journey, had sung together, *"Venite Adoramus, Venite Adoramus, Dominum"* (O come, let us adore him, O come, let us adore him, Christ the Lord). In that moment we were caught up in the Spirit, caught up in love, wonder, and praise, and worship happened. But it was not just the experience of true worship that made the moment unforgettable. It was that we had worshiped with the great company of heaven, and God had come down and inhabited our praise. That close encounter, that interchange between God and our small company of pilgrims, had made the time a holy time, and the exchange a holy one. And because of that we were not merely transfixed; we were transfigured in some small way into God's likeness, and, paradoxically enough, in and by the same act we had affirmed our lack of divinity, our creaturely nature. This was, is, and always will be the essence of true worship.

Amen

Wise Men Still Seek Him

Matthew 2:1-12

Staring at the Stars

Anyone who has every studied the sculpture and art of the ancient Near East will at some juncture have run across a particular common small household statue of a man. The man, with head inclined towards the heavens, has his eyes wide open and a look of wonder on his face. Both before, during, and after Jesus' day, all societies were agricultural, and thus they were all dependent on the heavens, on rain and sun, in order to live at all. Of course, this is true of us as well, but as the majority of us have become increasingly less tethered to the soil we have tended to forget this fact. It is no wonder that persons in those days constantly consulted the heavens ("from whence their help came"), the stars in their motions and configurations, the movement of the planets and of special astral events like comets, in order to discern when would be an opportune time to plow or allow the land to lie fallow, plant or pluck up. Indeed, one can read the *Farmer's Almanac* even to this day and get a sense of how closely prognostication is linked to an agrarian society like that of Jesus.

Astrologers, or *Magi* as they are called in our text (from which we get the word *magic*), were stargazers. They were not kings, but they were most definitely consultants to kings. The Magi constantly looked to the stars for help, for hope, for knowledge of the future, for truth. They did not believe the stars were mere inanimate matter; they believed they were likely to be supernatural beings — the heavenly hosts or angels. This is hardly surprising, since they saw them moving around in orderly patterns with the seasons of the year.

Our text in Matthew does not condemn these men for searching the stars, nor for following one large one in particular (which, oddly enough, considering its wandering pattern and its resting over the home of the Holy One, was more likely to be an angel than an actual star). It is significant, though, that the Magi had only the most general of understandings of what was going to transpire by consulting this source of knowledge. Their understanding is certainly enhanced tenfold when they arrive at the palace of King Herod and hear what the Scripture in Micah had foretold about the line of David, and of the Messiah being born in Bethlehem. There is perhaps a subtle polemic here, implying that the Word of God is far more revealing about such things than is the creation work of God.

There is a noteworthy contrast in the story between wicked King Herod, and the wise Magi, who, when warned in a dream against going back and reporting to Herod, go home by another way. The Magi sought the new King of the Jews in earnest, Herod sought him with evil intent, wanting to eliminate any rival to the throne. There is something to be learned from this. The Magi found what they sought in the manger, for they were earnest and honest seekers after the greatest truth of this world. Herod sought Jesus for self-seeking reasons but came up empty-handed. Herod was only interested in keeping what he thought was rightfully his. The wise men gave what was theirs in order to honor another and greater personage.

We are meant to think that the wise men gave their gifts as tokens of their worship of Christ, and as such they serve as harbingers of non-Jews who would come to worship King Jesus as well. But what strange birthday presents they offered Jesus.

Gifts Fit for a King?

One of my favorite short stories is by an author from Greensboro, North Carolina (not far from my hometown), whose pen name was O. Henry. It is entitled "The Gifts of the Magi." It is the poignant short story of a young couple very much in love, but very much without significant resources. The young man had a family heirloom pocketwatch, but had been unable to afford a chain for it. The young woman had long, beautiful hair but could not afford the stylish combs and clasps of the day used to hold up and properly display hair. Yet each one wished to give the other a special Christmas gift. Unbeknownst to the other, they set their plans in motion. The young man pawned his watch so he could buy some beautiful silver and gold hair clasps and combs. The young woman cut off and sold her beautiful hair so she could purchase that solid gold watch chain. When Christmas arrived, to both their utter surprise and dismay they had only gifts to give that were utterly useless on that day. But they realized that the sacrifices behind the expensive gifts showed how very deeply they loved one another — and so they had a happy Christmas after all.

In a way the story of those early Magi is much like this. They were not kings; and indeed, we are not told that there were three of them. This is a deduction based on the number of gifts they gave Jesus — but of course two, twenty, or two hundred individuals can all go in together and give three gifts. All we know is that there were more than one of these Magi. How had they come by such lavish gifts? Presumably they had obtained them from some royal court in the East, as a sort of consulting fee, or as rewards for successfully predicting some event. What is noteworthy is that all three of these gifts were associated with royalty — gold, a gift only a king could normally afford; frankincense, used in worship and in ceremonies to create an atmosphere of mystery and wonder; and myrrh, a spice used in the burial of kings, as an odor retardant in the winding sheet of the deceased. There has been much speculation about why these gifts were given to Jesus. Certainly they are gifts fit for a king, but they seem specifically designed for a king who had come, would reign and be worshiped, and who also would die, indeed be crucified as a king and be buried like one — with a huge amount of spices (see John 20). What should we make of this story, and what possible relevance does it have for us now? I am tempted to say, much in every way.

All Roads Lead to Bethlehem

There was a saying in antiquity: "All roads lead to Rome, the eternal city." But our Evangelist has another thought. In his view, all roads, and indeed all knowledge, even that found in the heavens, lead to Bethlehem and to Jesus. Jesus is, to put it one way, the fixed star around which heaven and earth revolve. He is the fulcrum or hinge of history, on which the whole story hangs. He is, as this story emphasizes, the only human being worthy of our worship, indeed, of the most elaborate forms of worship. *Epiphany* means "appearing," and one can say that this story is about Jesus' "coming out party," his becoming evident to those both near and far, high and low.

People in antiquity gave honor ratings to cities. Usually the bigger ones got higher honor ratings; the smaller, more out-of-the-way ones, lesser ratings. Bethlehem in Jesus' day was not even a one-stoplight town. It was a wide place in the road, near a bunch of sheep farms. It probably had no wayside inn at all, but that's a story for another day. Yet it had one great claim to fame before the time of Jesus: it was the city of David, and therefore was thought to be the city in which the great descendant of David, the Messiah, would also be born. Jesus lived in Bethlehem so short a time, due to King Herod's wrath, that he was never associated with the town thereafter — he was called Jesus of Nazareth, something that would hinder some from seeing Jesus in a royal light.

This story raises the question, what would we like to be remembered for? King Herod was remembered for his slaughtering the innocents, an act not out of character given that we know he executed members of his own family when he suspected they might usurp his throne. But the Magi were remembered for coming and worshiping Jesus and giving him the very best gifts they could muster. They disappear from the biblical record after they have worshiped Jesus. How do you wish to be remembered this year? Will it be all about getting things, or will it be about giving, and more importantly, will it be about the most important sort of giving — giving Jesus the worship he deserves? We could all do worse than follow in the footsteps of the Magi, and give lavishly to him in honor of his birth. The King Herods of this world will of course think that it should be all about them, but we do not have to follow their lead. As the Magi did, we can go home another way, preferably a way that does not lead to the halls of human power or conspicuous consumption. The road home, oddly enough, leads through a nowhere town called Bethlehem where God showed up incognito.

Amen

Excuse Me!

Proverbs 9:1-6, 13-18; Luke 14:1-6, 15-24

Table Manners

Growing up in the South, one grows accustomed to the habits of a culture in which politeness and gentility are stressed. "Yes, sir" and "Yes, ma'am" are standard fare, but perhaps at the dinner table more than anywhere else, we find such customs. One custom that was ingrained into me as a small child was to never leave the table without first asking to be excused by the host or hostess. In our parable for today, we have this same process functioning — only with a twist. The dinner guests are asking to be excused before they even taste any of the banquet!

So often this is the way we are as people, even as God's people. We make excuses, any excuse, to avoid doing what we are called and beckoned to do, before we even know the nature of what God is calling us to do or even attempt to do it. Since this parable speaks to all of us in our human situation, we will now examine it closely.

This parable, according to the Evangelist Luke, was told at the occasion of Jesus' dining with some of the religious elite — the Pharisees and the religious lawyers of his day. Doubtless they were curious to hear the teaching of this controversial preacher named Jesus. At one point in the banquet, one in the company remarked in a pious vein, "Blessed is he who shall dine in the Kingdom of God." The person who made this remark conceived of the Kingdom as something confined to the future, much as some people today talk as if God's blessings will only be available to us in heaven. By the term "Kingdom of God," the speaker was referring to the privilege

43

of participating in God's salvation, in God's community in the future. Now, it may be that this person was convinced that he, as a pious Jew, was assured of his slice of "pie in the sky." There seems to be a certain smugness going beyond confidence in his remark.

Yet Jesus, in response, told this parable that has as its message that those who were initially invited to come to the Kingdom to feast on God's gift of salvation may, in the end, fail to do so because they are not prepared to accept God's Kingdom on his timing and his terms. Not only so, but by contrast, those who were not initially invited, those whom the Pharisees might think ought not to be invited — the down and out, the poor, the simple, the harlots, the tax collectors — were being received into the Kingdom and sharing in it here and now. The last had become first, and the first last, or possibly even lost.

Flimsy Excuses

Jesus, in typical fashion, told his parable so it would fit in with what was customary and well-known in his day. When a man was going to hold a banquet, he would issue two invitations, one well in advance of the event, and another right at the time of the banquet itself so that those invited would be sure to "come and get it while it's hot." The sending out of the servant in the parable corresponds to the second, not the first, invitation. It is crucial to realize that the different people to whom the servant went had already been invited once, and had not previously refused the invitation. In many oriental cultures, refusing the second invitation was the worst slap in the face one could give a host.

The excuses offered by those who were invited are all pretty flimsy. The first person says that he is in the process of increasing his property and must go inspect it. Now, obviously, he could have done this at another time — but his field was more important to him than honoring the invitation. The second man, who is obviously rather well off, like the first, because he can afford to make expensive purchases, says that he has got five new teams of oxen and he wants to examine them. The clear implication is that he would rather see the faces of his beasts of burden than the face of his host! The third is the rudest of all. He does not ask to be excused, but simply says that he cannot come because he just married. The implication is that he cannot spare one night for a friend because he is so obsessed with his family affairs.

Now, some of this might seem a bit flimsy to you, and you may be saying that you would never make such excuses. But haven't we all done so at some point in our lives? In point of fact, it is still business preoccupations, worldly possessions, and domestic ties that make many refuse God's invitation to accept his gift of a place in the Kingdom, his gift of salvation. You would not believe some of the excuses I have heard from both Christians and non-Christians in this regard! One says, "I'm going to come to church just as soon as I get married and settle down." Another says, "Sunday is my only day to rest." They can't spare an hour for the Lord, as if going to church was hard work or a real burden. Another says, "I'll be there next Sunday if I can get up in time for the nine o'clock service." Or, "I'll come to your service, but I'm scared to go out at night." What kind of faith is it that refuses to trust God in the night as well as in the day? Or, "I'll come to church but I don't have a ride." How about, "It's too hot," or "It's too cold." "The seats are too hard." "The cushions aren't finished yet." "The lilies make me sneeze."

Excuses can be made about whether to become a Christian; whether to participate in worship; or whether to come to fellowship events. But to put it bluntly, the Lord knows the difference between excuses and legitimate reasons.

Banqueting with the Bad

In the parable, the host was livid, and he told his servants to go out and literally invite people in off the street. What an amazing sight that would have been. The lame lounging at a fancy table; the blind eating the bounty; the poor marveling at the majesty of a rich man's home. But Jesus is not simply trying to paint an interesting picture. He is saying to these Pharisees, *that is what the Kingdom of God is really like.* Poor and rich, black and white, young and old, healthy and sick, people from all walks of life together and finally on equal footing. Why? Because all are equal in the eyes of God if they have repented and believe in Jesus, his son.

As you know, however, Jesus' vision of the Kingdom was not limited to what will happen one day in the future. He was saying to his listeners, "This is what is happening now. Behold, I am bringing in the Kingdom." But the people he would have first called to the table — the religious leaders — had turned him down. And now he was inviting all those that the

Pharisees would have nothing to do with — the poor, sick, and sinners off the street. Jesus was the friend of all sinners. And the Pharisees knew it and taunted him.

Jesus knew that it was easy for devout Pharisees to become smug and secure, and to believe they had a place in the Kingdom. They were super-religious, or so they thought. They were fanatical about following the laws of the Old Testament in every detail. But in the course of this approach to religion, they were missing the Good News. They were missing God's servant, sent to tell them that the banquet was now being served. They had their excuses for not accepting God's invitation to the banquet. And thus they were in danger of missing the Kingdom altogether. They had their excuses for not taking up their crosses and following Jesus in the path of discipleship. But in the end, God will not ask you how good your ministers were, but how faithful you were in participating in the ministry.

Hanging by a Thread

There is a Danish fable that tells how a spider once slid down a filament from the rafters of a lofty barn and established himself on a lower level. There he spread his web, caught plenty of flies, and grew sleek and prosperous. One day, wandering about his premises, he saw the thread which stretched up into the unseen above him. "What is that for?" said the spider, and snapped it. And all his little house of life collapsed about him.

Sometimes we get so preoccupied with our activities, whether business or social or domestic, that we forget the Source of all such blessings and fail to heed his call. Our love for and glorifying in what God gives us comes to displace our love for and glorifying of the Lord himself. It is as Helmut Thielicke, the theologian, says in his book *The Waiting Father:* "The longer we are Christians, the more commonplace does this unheard of thing become. The miracle is taken for granted and the supernatural becomes second nature. We are a bit spoiled and coddled with this grace that is so easily piped into us by way of baptism and confirmation in the midst of our respectable Christian lives. And therefore, we can hardly appreciate the tremendous blessedness of that invitation. But Christian satiation is worse than hungry heathenism. It is not for nothing that the saying about 'Those who hunger and thirst' appears in the Sermon on the Mount."

It is when we become complacent about our faith that we then feel we can make excuses to God why we are not doing as we ought, not living as we ought, not supporting our church as we ought. But Jesus is saying to us, "The table is set, the dinner is waiting, the time to have fellowship with me and my people is now." The time to rest on our laurels is never.

If you have not accepted the first invitation to the Christian life, I hope you will soon do so. It you have accepted that call, hear now the second invitation of Jesus to the banqueting table. Do not make excuses. Let us continue to live as Christians whose faith bears fruit in good works, in God's work, and in faithful worship in service to Our Lord. We all are people who can live without excuses.

Amen

For Study and Meditation

"Transfigured"
(Isaiah 6, Revelation 4)

- Worship God through prayer, Scripture reading, or song. Listen to hymns or praise songs that offer glory and praise to God.
- Read through Psalm 84 aloud during your worship time, thanking and praising God.
- Write an original prayer of praise, compose a poem or song of praise, draw or paint a picture of praise, or spend time with God in nature. Worship him!

THOUGHTS FOR FURTHER MEDITATION

"Worship happens when the creature realizes he is not the Creator and bows down before and adores the one who is."

Ben Witherington III

"The chief aim of worship is that we be caught up in love, wonder, and praise of God, and in so doing get a glimpse of the heavenly worship that happens when and as we are worshiping."

Ben Witherington III

"The great thing and the only thing is to adore and to praise God."

Thomas Merton

"O Lord, that lends me life,
Lend me a heart replete with thankfulness."

William Shakespeare, *Henry VI*

"Wise Men Still Seek Him"
(Matthew 2:1-12)

◆ Meditate on Matthew 2:1-2. If you live in an area where the stars can be clearly seen, go outside at night and look at the sky. Reflect on the lavish gifts of the Magi. Ask God to reveal to you what you can give to him that you are holding back. Pray that he will help you to lay it at his feet.

◆ Pray about how God might be calling you to give of yourself. Ask him to reveal his plans for you and give you confidence to act. Each of us is uniquely gifted to serve the Lord in many ways. Pray with open hands and an open heart to receive!

◆ Serve the Lord in a new way this week. Look into opportunities at your church or in the area to share the gospel with others.

THOUGHTS FOR FURTHER REFLECTION

"Jesus is, to put it one way, the fixed star around which heaven and earth revolve. He is the fulcrum or hinge of history, on which the whole story hangs."

Ben Witherington III

"Everybody can be great. Because anybody can serve. You don't have to have a college degree to serve. You don't have to make your subject and your verb agree to serve. . . . You only need a heart full of grace. A soul generated by love."

Martin Luther King Jr.

"I am only one; but I am still one. I cannot do everything, but still I can do something; I will not refuse to do something I can do."

Helen Keller

"Excuse Me!"
(Proverbs 9:1-6; Luke 14:1-6, 15-24)

♦ Confess to God where you have made excuses to avoid doing what he has called you to do. Ask him for courage and strength to be the person he has called you to be.

♦ Ask God to reveal to you his desires for you. It may help to read stories in the Bible of God's faithfulness to others — for example, Noah, Moses, Ruth, Mary, Paul — in their obedience. As you meditate and consider these stories, reflect on times you have been obedient as well. Let yourself remember God's own faithfulness in these times, too. Write down those times as a reminder and encouragement.

♦ Pray for wisdom and willingness to go wherever God may lead.

THOUGHTS FOR FURTHER REFLECTION

"We make excuses, any excuse, to avoid doing what we are called and beckoned to do, before we even know the nature of what God is calling us to do or even attempt to do it."

Ben Witherington III

"O God, be all my love, all my hope, all my striving; let my thoughts and words flow from you, my daily life be in you, and every breath I take be for you."

John Cassian

"O Lord Jesus Christ . . . save us from the error of wishing to admire you instead of being willing to follow you and to resemble you."

Søren Kierkegaard

For Study and Meditation

"Thy will be done, though in my undoing."

Sir Thomas Browne

"O Lord, let us not live to be useless, for Christ's sake."

John Wesley

LENT

The Lengthening of the Light

"To Err Is Human, to Forgive . . ."

Matthew 18:21-35; Romans 4:1-8

Unforgiving

John Wesley was having a heated discussion with a judge of the assize. The judge was adamant about the seriousness of his task of judging. Wesley was reminding him that justice needed to be tempered with mercy, and indeed a judge even needed to be prepared to offer forgiveness. The judge stiffly replied, "I never forgive, sir." Wesley, in his usual direct and no-nonsense manner, replied, immediately, "Then I hope you never sin, sir."

Forgiveness is in some ways the ultimate litmus test of Christian character, the test of Christ-likeness, for we serve a savior who even from the Cross prayed for the forgiveness of his tormentors, and, as Henri Nouwen reminds us, it was only after he said, "Father, forgive them, for they do not realize what they are doing," that he was able to go on and say to that same heavenly Father, "Into your hands I commend my spirit."

We serve a savior who, on the very night in which he was betrayed, deserted, and denied three times, celebrated Passover with the same persons who committed these acts, and shared tokens and pledges of forgiveness in the form of bread and wine, in advance of their sinning and in advance of his costly work of redemption on the Cross. Like the father in the Parable of the Prodigal Son, Jesus comes running, offering forgiveness even before we are prepared to repent or confess or be absolved. If this is our example, what, then, is required of us as followers of Jesus?

The Meaning of Forgiveness

The Greek verb *aphiemi* has the following core meanings: 1) to remit a debt, referring to something owed rather than an optional gift; 2) to allow to be, to tolerate; 3) to leave behind, forsake, let go, dismiss (it is even the verb used for "to divorce"); 4) to cancel. I would suggest that all these meanings and additional collateral concepts come into play when the matter is Christian forgiveness.

Forgiveness therefore involves the following: 1) an unconditional release of the other person who has hurt you; 2) an actual telling them that they are forgiven; and 3) most difficult of all, a good faith effort at reconciliation with the person. But there is more.

Jesus in his teaching in the Sermon on the Mount indicates clearly that the "wronging" party has an obligation to seek forgiveness from the one who has "something against you." Jesus even advises in Matthew 5:23-24 to "leave your gift or praise at the altar for another time and go, if your brother or sister has something against you, and be reconciled to them first." Think of that — you are not in a condition to offer praise or gifts at the altar until you make the effort at making amends and reconciliation.

This wisdom, of course, is counterintuitive, and indeed it is counter-cultural. Today in our legal system we set up structures to protect "victims" from ever having to deal with the wronging party again, and doubtless this is sometimes necessary. But, frankly, the Christian community cannot make this a principle of operation, not least because we live in a world where hardly anyone wants to take responsibility for their own actions: they would rather claim to be victims of someone else's act. Jesus' direct command to us is meant to set in motion a community ethic in which not just in praying to God, but also in our actions with each other, we seek forgiveness.

The Need for and Effects of Forgiveness

Douglas Steere in his wonderful book *Dimensions of Prayer* says this: "Forgiveness is a condition in which the sin of the past is not altered, nor its inevitable consequences changed. Rather in forgiveness a fresh act is added to those of the past, which restores the broken relationship and opens the way for the one who forgives and the one who is forgiven to meet and communicate deeply with each other in the present and future. Thus forgiveness heals the past, though the scars remain and the consequences go on."

Forgiveness is not a mere option for a Christian; it is an obligation. Unforgiveness is a serious sin, which shrivels up the human soul. So much is it an obligation that we forgive that in the Lord's Prayer we are informed that we are forgiven just as much as we forgive. The vertical receiving of forgiveness in some way is connected to and hinges on our being prepared to forgive those who have wronged us. But real forgiveness requires a grace and a graciousness that goes beyond normal human abilities.

One of my spiritual heroes has been Corrie ten Boom, a Dutch Christian woman who survived the Nazi death camp known as Ravensbruck, but not without great cost. She had the horrific experience of watching helplessly as her sister was beaten to death by a death camp guard. Seething with anger as her sister lay on the morgue slab, she heard her sister Betsy say with her dying breath: "No hate, Corrie, only love. No hate, Corrie, only love." It was a tall order to fulfill that last request.

Many years later, when Corrie was giving her testimony at a Christian worship event in Germany, a man came up to her. He approached her quietly and said, "You will perhaps not remember or recognize me, but I too was in Ravensbruck; in fact, unfortunately I was the guard who beat your sister to death. I have asked the Lord to forgive me but I must also ask you if you will do so." With tears welling up in her eyes Corrie's immediate, instinctive response was to say "I cannot, I cannot; but give me your phone number and I will pray about it." In that moment of recognition she had had a flashback and saw her sister dying, and anger had overtaken her just as the memory had.

Some days later, after lots of wrestling in prayer, Corrie called the man and told him: "This act of forgiveness is not really humanly possible for me, and yet God has given me the grace to forgive you and so I do, and I release you from the burden of your guilt for this." This was not a natural act; it was supernatural and it benefited both the giver and the receiver of forgiveness.

The Peter Principle

In our text for today, we have heard Peter's inquiry with Jesus about the matter of forgiveness. Doubtless Peter thought that he was being exceed-

ingly charitable when he suggested that perhaps he should forgive someone seven times. After all, seven in that culture was the number for perfection or completion.

But Jesus, in turn, replied that in fact *unlimited* acts of forgiveness are
expected of his disciples — seven times seventy doesn't mean, "Quit after
490 times!" It means, "Go on to perfection, and unlimited forgiveness."
Again, this can only be done by the grace of God.

Then notice that Jesus immediately goes on to tell a parable in which
he says that if we are unforgiving like the unmerciful servant, God will require of us payment for our sins! If having received from Christ so great a
forgiveness we are not in turn prepared to forgive the lesser sins we have
suffered, there will be consequences. The other meaning of *aphiemi* will
come into play — the remittance of the debt owed, required of you by
God, will come due!

And here we need to speak for a moment about "truth or consequences." We would like to think we live in a no-fault universe, but we do
not. Time and again both Jesus and Paul warn their own followers that
there will be consequences for their misbehavior. Salvation by grace
through faith does not rule this out in any way. Indeed, there comes a point
where both Jesus and Paul stress that repeated or habitual bad behavior,
including unforgiveness, can keep their followers out of the eternal kingdom that is yet to come.

Paul was worried about this no-fault sort of religion that misunder-
stands forgiveness and holiness when he asked the question: "Should we
sin, so grace may abound?" His answer was a terse and vehement, "Absolutely not." Unfortunately, the church all too often cultivates a climate of
forgiveness without repentance or amendment of life being required.

We may even make the mistake of assuming that this is the nature of
God's grace — it is unconditionally given without any requirements attached. When I was at Carolina I once heard the testimony of a young
Christian woman who thought it worked like that. She said, "The way I see
it, I like committing sins and God likes forgiving sins. It all works out very
well." This is a huge mistake — what God requires of his children is holiness of heart and life. Forgiveness neither annuls the need for this nor in
some way trumps it.

Paul on Pardon

It is interesting that in the one place in Paul's letters where he actually talks about this matter directly, in Romans 4:1-8, it comes precisely in the midst of his discussion of righteousness, in this case the right standing Abraham obtained with God through faith. We need to hear this text at this juncture. It is important both for what it does say, and for what it does not say. For example, it says nothing about Christ's righteousness being credited to us. It says that the credit and debit ledger involves two Abraham entries: Abraham's faith or trust in God, and Abraham's right standing, which we should see as a gift from God. "Abraham trusted God and it was credited as right standing." This was obviously not in lieu of his going on to be righteous in behavior.

As anyone who reads Genesis 12–21 will know, God repeatedly holds Abraham's feet to the fire for various sins and tests him mightily. Furthermore, when Paul speaks of right standing or credit apart from works of the law, he has in mind works of the Mosaic law, not activities or work or good behavior in general. Indeed, Paul will go on to insist in Galatians 5–6 that right behavior is required of Christians, indeed, they are to keep the law of Christ, which among other things means avoiding all the vices on the vice list in Galatians 5. Otherwise, says Paul, they shall not enter the eschatological dominion of God in the future. Forgiveness obviously is not a blank check getting one into eternity.

In fact, Paul in that same Romans 4 text goes on to quote Psalm 32:1-2 to the following effect: "Blessed are those whose transgressions are forgiven, whose sins are covered. Blessed are those whose sin God never counts against them." But who are these people? They are those who live by trust in God as Abraham did, and who repent of their sins and live in an upright manner as Abraham was taught to do, sometimes even taught by hard experience.

That quote from the Psalms is interesting on three accounts: 1) Paul makes a distinction between sins and transgressions — the latter involves a willful violation of a known law. Paul has set up this distinction in his discussion in Romans 2–4 about those who are sinners apart from the law. The Mosaic law turned sin into transgression — a more serious matter. 2) Paul says that the atoning death of Jesus covers both sin and transgression. 3) This is something new, since, as Acts 13:39 puts it, "Through him everyone who believes is justified from everything you could not be justified from by the law of Moses." In short, there were sins with a high hand, deliberate sins for which there was no atonement in Old Testament law. One simply had to throw oneself on the mercy of God as David did in Psalm 51.

One more set of New Testament passages worth considering are several gospel texts. As is well known, the Lukan word of Jesus from the cross is, "Father, forgive them, for they know not what they do." This verse fits well with other Lukan texts in Acts that deal with the problem of ignorance and its relationship to forgiveness. For example, we may think of Acts 3:17, in which Peter says, "I know you acted in ignorance." Ignorance is apparently a mitigating factor which should make forgiveness easier to come by.

This connection between knowledge, deliberate sin, and judgment on the one hand and ignorance, forgiveness, and release from punishment on the other is worth pondering for its practical implications. It is also an important theme in the early speeches in Acts, in which, when the Christian speaker is asked how one may remedy one's lost condition, the standard reply is, "Repent, be baptized for the release of your sins," or, "Repent, turn to God so sins may be released, wiped out." Repentance, then, seems to be a key to being released from sin and its consequence. An offended party can forgive, and indeed needs to forgive, for their own spiritual well-being, but this act in itself is not enough for the offending person to be released from their sins. Repentance is also necessary.

Forgiveness in the Old Testament looks quite different from forgiveness in the New due mainly to the all-encompassing death of Jesus, which covers every type of sin, and indeed, as various New Testament texts make clear, covers the sins of the world. His death is sufficient for all, but only efficient for those who trust as Abraham did in God and so are saved by grace through faith. Christ's death covers both premeditated and spontaneous sin, both sins of ignorance and sins of knowledge, both sins of commission and sins of omission. How, then, should all this theology affect our practice of ministry and of Christian living?

The Practice of the Gift of Forgiveness

Perhaps we could begin by asking practical questions. What are your obstacles to forgiving others? Are you overly sensitive and feel that someone has done you a much greater wrong than in fact they have done, and therefore it becomes difficult to forgive them? Have you so demonized the person who hurt you that you cannot find a way to build a bridge back to them offering release and reconciliation? Or perhaps are you like those who think they have never committed a major sin, and so feel you are in a morally superior position?

Perhaps, however, you are a person who feels so unworthy and has such low self-esteem that you have trouble receiving any gift, much less forgiveness. To you the good news needs to be told that forgiveness is not about one's worthiness to receive it but rather the graciousness and worth of the one who gives it.

If any of these things describes you, then hear the Good News — God's transforming grace can change your heart of stone into a heart of compassion. God's transforming grace can reassure you that you are a person of sacred worth, and you can receive forgiveness. God's transforming grace can enable you to forgive even when in your own strength you cannot pull it off. God's transforming grace can make clear to you that all have sinned and fallen short of God's glory, so there is no place in the body of Christ for an attitude of moral superiority that looks down on others. This is not holiness; it is what Jesus calls hypocrisy — the seeing and critiquing and trying even to extract specks from others' eyes and ignoring the plank in your own.

Lastly, forgiveness has an integral relationship to the sacraments, especially the Lord's Supper. After the Civil War in a Presbyterian church in Richmond, Virginia, a worship service was being held to help heal the wounds that were festering after the war. It was a service that concluded with the service of holy communion. This church was attended both by former slave owners and former slaves, and the practice before and during the war was that the African Americans would sit in the balcony and would come to communion separately after all the white people who sat downstairs. There were, then, two calls for communion. But on this Sunday on the first invitation to communion an elderly African American man started down the aisle, and a gasp went up in the congregation. Quickly an elderly white man slipped into the aisle and hooked his arm into that of the African American man, and they went forward and took communion together. The man was Robert E. Lee, the general-in-chief of the Southern army, who had been in favor of emancipation before the war, but could not fight against his own home of Virginia. Now, after the war, he was resolved to work for the healing of the wounds. On that day in Richmond, at the altar of that church, forgiveness began to be given and received.

Once received from God, forgiveness is meant to be shared with others. Here is a key to breaking the cycle of violence and hatred and prejudice. As Alexander Pope rightly said long ago: "To err is human, to forgive divine."

Amen

Eternal Treasures in Earthen Vessels

2 Corinthians 4:7-18

Preached in Bulawayo, Zimbabwe, at the first joint
worship service of Shona and Ndebele Christians

The World of the Apostle

We live in a hurting world, a fact that Paul knew well and knew personally. He was stoned, shipwrecked, imprisoned, whipped several times within an inch of his life. He was always in trouble or getting out of trouble. If his resume were sent to the Board of Ordained Ministry in my denomination, I doubt anyone would ordain or appoint him today. That resume looked more like a post-office poster of a wanted criminal. But humanly speaking, if Paul had not done what he did as the apostle to the Gentiles, it is doubtful we would be here today in this worship service, entirely or almost entirely populated by non-Jews. The remarkable thing about this is that while the world did not cease to be a hurting place, that hurting in no way stopped the gospel, for, as 2 Corinthians tells us, God's power is made perfect in our weakness; his grace is sufficient for us.

Some thirty years ago when I was ordained, one of the presiding bishops at Lake Junaluska, North Carolina, was Kenneth Goodson. In his ordination sermon, entitled "Stewards of the Mysteries of God," Bishop Goodson told the story of when he was a minister in a large church in Winston-Salem and most of his senior high youth group had gone off on a mission project to Mexico. A phone call came late one night to Pastor Goodson telling him that a truck with no lights had smashed into the church bus and more than a few of his high school parishioners had been instantly killed. The bishop recounted how he sat on his front porch that night, looking up at the stars and trying to think of the words he would say to each of the parents he now had to call and convey the news of this tragedy. How do we cope with this sort of tragedy without trivializing it? How do we deal with pain that will not go away, or evil that lurks at every turn, or a world filled with suffering, sorrow, disease, decay, and death? Is it really possible that God could use our suffering, and indeed our weaknesses, to bear witness to the truth and love that is God?

Yes, indeed, is Paul's answer, for that is how God changed the world in the first place, through the seemingly tragic and unjust death of Jesus. Even in Jesus' case was it true that God's power was made perfect and evident through human weakness, suffering, and even death. What we learn from that story is that God's Yes to life is louder than death's No, and, likewise, greater is he who is in us, than anything the world can throw at us.

Corrie ten Boom tells the story of being confronted in Ravensbruck death camp during World War II by a Jewish woman who had been a concert violinist, and who had had to endure a sadistic guard deliberately breaking her fingers when he found out her profession. Corrie had been speaking to her fellow inmates about the love of God, which transcended their situation and could even transform it, and this was finally too much for the violinist. She confronted Corrie and asked, "How can you believe in a God of love who would allow this to happen to my fingers?" It was a searching question and Corrie did not want to treat it disrespectfully. She simply said, "I do not know why this has happened to you, but my faith is not based on the mysteries of what I do not know or understand. It is based on what I do know. What I know is that no pit is so deep, that God's love is not deeper still." This is indeed the Christian answer, which does not deny the reality of evil or suffering or wickedness but insists that there is a great power in the universe, a power for love and for the good.

The Wounds of the Apostle

Paul makes an interesting and direct contrast in our text between what is true of the believer inwardly and what is true of them outwardly in their bodies. Paul says that outwardly we are wasting away, while inwardly we are being renewed day after day. I once had a college English teacher from the U.K. who came into class looking disheveled one day and said in his best Oxbridge accent, "There are days in life after forty when you realize that your body is your mortal enemy." Indeed there are; in fact, such light may dawn before age forty. I remember playing a basketball game (the game I played most in my youth) when I was nearing forty, and there was a juncture in the game at which I had a chance to go up and lay the ball off the rim, or at least I thought so, since I had been able to do this when young, being a good leaper. My mind told me, "Go ahead, go for it!" However, my mind was obviously more youthful than my body — my mind was, in fact, writing checks my body couldn't cash! Outwardly I was wasting away, but inwardly being renewed day by day.

According to Paul, the one part of the Christian not being renewed in this life is the physical body. The mind, the heart, the will, the emotions, the spirit, all the inner self is being renewed already, but the body must await the resurrection, our own personal Easter experience. Even if by some miracle God restores us after an accident or severe illness, we will still go on to die. This body is still terminal unless the Lord returns before we die. Accordingly, it can be said that the body is the chink in the Christian's armor, which may partially explain why Paul focuses so much on the sins of the flesh in his letters.

It is one of the great strengths of Christianity that it does not deny the reality or power of suffering and evil. But in Christ suffering is both transfigured and transcended. In other words, the reality of Christ and his grace is more profound than the reality of our weakness and vulnerabilities to suffering and evil. We must learn from the example of Corrie ten Boom and not settle for glib dismissals of suffering or evil but rather emphasize the greater reality of Christ and his resurrection power.

The Word of the Apostle

Paul says that the relationship between the inner and the outer person is like an eternal treasure in an earthen vessel. Since Paul goes on to speak about light shining in the darkness, it appears he is thinking about a hand lamp into which oil is poured and a wick is inserted and lit, shedding light in the darkness. These hand lamps were the ancient equivalent of flashlights, and the interesting thing about them is that it is precisely because the pottery is so thin and fragile that more light got out. So it is with us as well. We are visible, vulnerable light containers, such that when people look at our lives if they see strength in the midst of weakness, light in the midst of darkness, God's love in the midst of imperfections and flaws, they will know that "the all-surpassing power is from God, not from us." That eternal treasure, that life-giving light within us, keeps strengthening us and revivifying and energizing us.

When we lived in northeast Ohio for eleven years there was a lot of snow, and a lot of salted roads, and as a result a lot of cars rusted out all around the rims of the doors and front and rear grill work. Sometimes this was so much the case that one wondered how a rusty old rambling wreck could even be moving down the road. Then one remembered that there was such a thing as a Die Hard battery that kept charging and charging despite the outward condition of the vehicle. What Paul is describing is rather like that. Christians have a Die Hard battery within them, the living presence of Christ, and his life and light, such that even though they are outwardly decaying and getting older, inwardly they are being renewed day by day. And this leads, or can lead, to a remarkable change of attitude.

A Christian who realizes he or she has an eternal treasure in this all-too-mortal vessel is a person who should have an unconquerable spirit, not least because we remember that Christ overcame death through resurrection. Such a person should be able to live as a victor rather than a victim even in our dark and dangerous world. We can say with St. Paul, "I may be knocked down, but not knocked out, I may be beaten but not defeated." A Christian has no more control than anyone else over all of the things that will happen to them in life, no matter how secluded an existence they may live. Suffering and disease are often not predictable and often are no good barometer of the degree of a person's faith or lack thereof. Were that the case Paul would have ranked as a very poor Christian, since he was constantly suffering, and God even told him that he was not going to take his thorn in the flesh out of his flesh.

No, we cannot control our circumstances, but we can control how we will react to them by the grace of God. When life throws you a curveball, will you recognize it and swing away, or will you complain it's an unfair pitch? You have a choice. Will you be a victim or will you be a victor? You have a choice as to how you will respond to sorrow, suffering, persecution, disease, decay and death just as Paul did. You have an eternal resource, a great treasure that you can draw upon so as to be a light in a very dark and dangerous world. I would stress that we do have a promise from Paul that neither height nor depth, nor powers nor principalities, nor things present nor things to come, nor anything in all of creation can separate us from the love of God in Christ within us. So we might as well be flawed vessels who let the light within shine through us so people can see that the power comes from God.

The story is told about an Indian servant who regularly went to the Ganges to draw water in two earthen vessels attached to a yoke. The servant worked in the palace of a great king. One day when the servant went to the river he noticed that the two water vessels were actually speaking to each other. The vessel on the right side of the yoke was flawed, had a crack in it which led to a small amount of water leaking out along the path to the palace. This vessel complained, "If only I could be like the other vessel, who every day serves the King well by bringing a full vessel of water to the house." Hearing this the servant interrupted and said: "Have you not, looking along your side of the path leading up to the house? Have you not noticed that only on your side of the house are there beautiful flowers, which I can pick and bring to the Queen each day? Can you not see that you are even more useful as a flawed vessel because not only do you bring water to the house, but also you have provided flowers for the royal family?"

We are all of us like that flawed vessel, and yet by allowing ourselves to be used as we are, the great King is served well, for his power and purposes and plans are made perfect in and through our weaknesses. Only by dying could Jesus rise to new resurrection life that was far better and more powerful than the life he had before. So it is, and so it shall be for us as well.

Amen

Grounds for Differences

Ezekiel 17:1-10, 22-24; Mark 4:1-20

Parables are similes, or analogies, or illustrations taken from the natural world or from common experience to make a religious point. Jesus was by no means the first to use them. Jewish prophets and teachers had been doing so for centuries, as our lesson from Ezekiel for this morning shows. Yet Jesus was apparently well known for teaching in parables, and thus Matthew, Mark, and Luke include a good number of these likeable analogies. Today we are going to examine in detail one of the more significant and crucial of the parables, the Parable of the Sower.

Setting the Stage

Whenever we study the Bible, it is critical that we first try to see what the text meant in its original setting, as heard by the audience to which Jesus delivered it, before we try to discover what it means for us today.

Our text tells us that Jesus was teaching by a lake, presumably the Sea of Galilee, and a huge crowd was gathered around him. So great was the crowd that Jesus had to get into a boat and speak to them from offshore. Jesus was near the point in his ministry at which he had his largest following.

As with the story of the feeding of the five thousand, we are dealing with a crowd of great proportions. Yet Jesus was not like many preachers today. He did not believe that just because he had a huge crowd following to hear him, he also had a large faithful following that would stick with him through thick and thin. Indeed, he told the Parable of the Sower to this huge crowd, and it is a parable that in part contradicts such naïve optimism. Had Jesus been like others, he might well have said, "Look how fruitful my ministry is!" Instead, he is saying there are many failures as well as some successes. Jesus experienced both failure and success in his ministry. Indeed, at one point even the Twelve deserted him, and thus there is no reason for any other minister to expect it to be otherwise.

Jesus knew that it was easy for listeners to get distracted, so he began his teaching of this and other parables with the word "Listen," or "Now hear this." "Wake up now. I'm going to tell you something important, so pay attention." Yes, even Jesus, as great a preacher as he was, had to exhort his audience to listen at times. If we read the Book of Acts, at least on one occasion St. Paul had a young man fall asleep during one of his preaching engagements. If it happened to Jesus and Paul, a modern preacher should have no delusions about his or her own preaching.

Sow Far, Sow Good

After grabbing their attention, Jesus goes on to use an illustration drawn from everyday farm life — the story of a sower. Doubtless, many of you can remember a day when planting seeds meant throwing them out by hand, and often this is still the case. In Jesus' day it was not common to be selective in sowing the seeds. A farmer was so desperate for a crop, he would use every inch of soil available, good and bad, hoping to have some results. Thus, the sower disperses the seed, and some of it falls on rocky soil, some falls on the roadside, and some falls on weed-infested ground. But some falls on good soil.

The seed that fell on the road could not even get into the ground; it lay on top and was eaten by the birds. The seed that fell on rocky soil grew a little but because the soil was not very deep, when it grew it could not put down sufficient roots for water. So when the sun came out, the plant dried up.

The seed that fell on ground infested with weeds and thorns had too much competition. This competition choked and strangled the new plants which never bore grain.

But the seed that fell on good soil produced beyond the farmer's wildest dreams. A sevenfold yield was considered a good harvest in Jesus' day. Thus, a thirty-, sixty-, or hundredfold yield would be quite a miraculous harvest. Despite all the failures, the successes were so good and bountiful that it made up for all the wasted efforts. "He who has ears to hear let him hear and learn from this example," says Jesus. What, then, does this say to us as Christians today?

The Good News

This is a text that realistically portrays both the Good News and the bad news. The Good News is that God is in our midst spreading his Word. He is planting seeds in human hearts that lead to changed lives. The Kingdom of God has come into our midst. And into the lives that are receiving it, fruit is being borne, far beyond the limits of our expectations. This is true because it is not merely humans who are planting the seed of the Word of God, not merely human preachers and prophets, but God working through them, with them, and also without them.

Thus, this parable can be seen as a word of encouragement to all of Jesus' disciples, both past and present, to never give up hope as they bear witness to the Word. Eventually, the Word will not fall on deaf ears, but on receptive hearts, and great will be the change that is wrought therein. The great successes make all the efforts, even those that seem to fail, worthwhile.

You may remember the famous story in the Old Testament in which a great man of God bargains with God saying, "Lord, you have said you will destroy this town, but if there are only 100 righteous people, will you spare this town?" And the Lord says, "Yes!" The man asks again, "What if there are only ten righteous?" And again, the Lord says, "Yes, I will spare the town." Finally, he challenges, "If only five righteous?"

And again the Lord says, "Yes." The point is clear that God is willing to expend great energies or restrain from great actions for the sake of only a few converts or righteous ones. So it was with Jesus, who though often thronged by crowds, chose only a few good people to carry on where he left off. We are here today because the first disciples did carry on.

Sometimes as Christians we get down in the dumps about the state of our church or the world. A Christian once put it humorously in a limerick:

God's word made a perfect beginning;
Man spoiled the creation by sinning.

70

> We know that the story
> Will end in God's Glory,
> But at present the other side's winning.

Yet this parable tells us that in spite of various apparent failures, God is still winning. The church is still saving souls. Jesus' disciples are still finding good soil in which to plant the seed, and thus our witness must go on.

The Rest of the Story . . .

But along with the Good News, there is also the bad news, and it tells us much about ourselves. The main distinctive feature about this parable is the different sorts of soils. That is where the emphasis lies. Jesus is saying that whether the Word is received, and to what degree it is received, depends on the receiver. In each case, the sower, God or his missionaries, is the same. In each case, the seed, God's Word, is the same. The difference is in the soil. This is why Jesus says, "Whoever has ears for this message, please hear it." Jesus is implying that there are some who do not hear the message. This is why Paul says that the unspiritual cannot receive or understand spiritual truths. One must first have God's Spirit within.

Some people's hearts are like an asphalt road, as hard as can be, not open to allow anything in from outside, especially not God's Word. Others are willing to listen a little to God's Word and a little fruit comes of it, but when it comes to taking up their cross and being responsible and helpful disciples in the church, the enthusiasm fails. Now still other people do not give God's Word the attention, time, and devotion it deserves. These people allow outside forces like work, pleasure, friends, sports, TV, and so on to distract them and draw them away from the Word so that the Word has to compete against numerous other forces. Sometimes these and other forces completely choke off and destroy our Christian growth and life. But then, too, there are those who hear God's Word and really take it to heart and apply it to their lives.

The question for us is, What sort of soil are we? What sort of listeners to God's Word are we? We can turn off the preacher altogether, and let our mind wander, and the words will fall on deaf ears. We can listen only with our ears as often happens in polite conversation, and the Word will go in one ear and out the other. Or we can listen with our minds only, and agree to what is said mentally but fail to act, fail to live out this truth. Or we can listen as though our eternal life depends on it. And so it does.

Jesus is saying, "Now hear this! The enemy is approaching. He is threatening to distract and disarm you, to steal your heart away. Are you armed and prepared? Do you know what to do in such a state of spiritual emergency? Have you the Word of God in your heart? Are you responding to it with your mind, body, spirit, emotions, lifestyle, and ethical conduct?"

And So?

A great Lutheran preacher of the twentieth century, Helmut Thielicke, concluded a sermon on this passage in this way:

> Jesus is never interested in counting and statistics. He always puts us to work. He says, "Weed out the thorns: see to it that the seed does not fall on the path. Be careful lest you be people so shallow that the Word cannot take root." Jesus says, "Be good soil." And that means hold on to the Word in stillness. Get rid of the hardness and callousness. Don't squeeze God into a few cracks and crevices of your day's business. But give him a space of daily quiet and don't avoid repentance. Work out your own salvation with fear and trembling. For God cannot be had cheaply. You come to God only if you allow yourself to be mobilized, and if you march. This is not easy, and it means saying good-bye to many things. But this is the only way to find his peace. No battle, no cross, no crown. He who does not toil and sweat, and does not daily fall in line for service to God is exposing his inner man to decay.

God's grace is not cheap grace. You must pay for it with all you are and all you have. You can loaf your way into hell, but the Kingdom of Heaven can only be seized by force. It is an exciting thing to be a Christian!

It is also a great truth that even if a person be rocky soil now, with God's grace he or she can be cultivated and become good soil tomorrow. And thus we must never give up on the lost. Jesus is saying, "Now hear this — I want you. The Kingdom of God is at hand. There is work to be done. There will be failures and successes. But the work shall bear fruit."

Amen

Death Be Not Proud

Philippians 1:12-26; 1 Corinthians 15:54-58; 2 Timothy 4:6-8

Deadly Approaches to Death

When all is said and done, there are only a few ways we humans can react to death. We can recognize it as a fact, and so let it dominate our thinking that it casts a shadow on all life, leaving nothing without the taint of its limiting nature. A person in this frame of mind will likely think that since death is a fact, then there is no real purpose or reason for doing anything. And further, there is no reason for refraining from doing all sorts of things. In such a worldview, the universe is seen as cruel and dangerous. Or perhaps life is seen as a beautiful but meaningless thing that cannot be counted on. In such a world there is no eternal significance. In such a world, nothing lasts for long, let alone forever.

A person who believes in this manner is called a nihilist or an existentialist. A person who truly believes that this is the way the world really works has a handful of options. First, he or she can commit suicide. Second, he or she can fight death all the way, taking the advice of the poet Dylan Thomas, who said, "Do not go gentle into that good night; /Rage, rage against the dying of the light!" Third, he or she can accept death as a fact, and the meaninglessness of existence as a result of that fact, and spend life trying to ignore death's reality by trying every new thing, and indulging in every new pleasure, and creating one's own happiness and meaning in life. This is commonly called hedonism. A hedonist says to us, "Since we all have to die, we might as well enjoy life as long as we can."

Fourth, there will be a few people as well who will talk idealistically of human togetherness and living for the common good. Some will run for office; others will work for social organizations; and most will try to make a name in this life since they do not believe in the next. All will have a strong urge to feel that their life has mattered. For instance, the Earl of Southampton begged Shakespeare, "Make me immortal in your verse," referring to Shakespeare's sonnets.

Finally, there are those who believe in reincarnation. For some of them, this life is useless, plagued by bad karma, and they can hardly wait to go on to the next.

The one thing shared in common by all five of these approaches to death — suicide, anger, hedonism, self-idolatry, reincarnation — is that these people all think that death is the end of all, the terminus, the brick wall that cannot be avoided but rather will necessarily be encountered in a head-on collision.

Probably most of you know someone that fits one of these descriptions. They honestly believe death is the end of everything, and that all one can hope for in life is a little happiness. Thus, happiness and pleasure have become the reason for living. Such people live, as the Apostle Paul puts it, as "people without hope." How very different is any of this from a Christian approach to death — and thus to life!

A Loved One Gone, but Not Lost

About five years ago I was at a funeral of the mother of a close friend of mine. I must say that her funeral service was one of the most joyful worship services I have ever attended. We sang great hymns like "Joyful, Joyful We Adore Thee" and "Praise to the Lord, the Almighty, the King of Creation." And we were rejoicing in earnest.

Why were we rejoicing when a wonderful Christian woman, who was greatly loved by her family and friends, had just died a painful death from cancer? I can assure you it was not because we were happy to see her go! It was because we knew that this woman, who had lived her life in accordance with the will of her Master, Jesus Christ, had gone to be with her Lord. There could be no greater blessing or more wonderful thing for her.

We knew that though we had temporarily lost sight of her, she had gained the end she had sought all her life — perfect fellowship with her Lord. We did not grieve, as Paul says, as the heathens do who have no hope.

We rejoiced. We realized that if we grieved too much it would be because of our own loss, not hers. Surely she was much better off with the Lord than in a hospital bed suffering the pains of cancer.

For a real Christian, grieving should not be overdone, lest it merely turn into feeling sorry for ourselves. But we should shed real tears for those who die without accepting Jesus Christ. For in that case, our loss and theirs is permanent.

I have suggested in telling this story a bit of how we as Christians should approach death. But there is more to be said. Christians should realize and recognize death for what it is. Death is horrible and often painful. Do not let anyone tell you that it is a perfectly natural process like eating and breathing. If any of you have ever been close to death, you will remember the extreme fear or dread you felt. The truth is that our whole being tells us that death is anything but natural. It is not like going to sleep. Apart from those who are in Christ, death is the end of life, not the refresher or restorer of life as sleep can be. It is cold; it is hard; it is ugly. Not only our natural reaction but Scripture itself tells us that death is anything but natural. Human death is a result of human sin — the consequence of our rebellion against the Lord of Life.

Contemplate again Christ hanging on a cross bearing the sins of the world. Death is the price we have long been paying for our sins. It is the ultimate manifestation of all that is evil and ugly. It is the end of that great, good gift of God — life. Were it not for Jesus Christ, death would be final, and rightly so. It is through his death that a Christian is restored to life.

A Christian can rejoice because he or she knows that there is something and someone more powerful than death in this world. What is it? The power of God and his love which acts in Jesus Christ. Because Jesus has died for our sins, and because Jesus went through death and triumphed in his bodily resurrection, we know that, "Greater is he who is in us, than he who is in the world." We know that "neither death nor life, nor angels nor princes, nor things that are, nor things to come, nor height nor depth, nor any created thing, can ever come between us and this powerful love of God which raised Jesus from death."

Death Be Not Proud

As Christians, then, we know how horrid death is. But we also know that it will not have the last word. The word of God's gift of eternal life and resurrection of the body in and through Jesus Christ — that is the last word. We know that this life is only the first installment of life for Christians. Further, we know that since death does not have the last word, then what we do in this life matters. As Paul puts it, "Death is swallowed up in victory. Death, where is your victory? Death, where is your sting?"

Let us thank God for giving us the victory through our Lord Jesus Christ. Never give in and never admit defeat. Keep on working at the Lord's work always. Know that in the Lord you cannot be laboring in vain. All is not vanity for the Christian. Hear the words of the great English poet John Donne:

> Death be not proud, though some have called thee
> Mighty and dreadful, for thou art not so;
> For those whom thou thinkest thou dost overthrow,
> Die not, poor death, nor yet canst thou kill me:
> From rest and sleep, which but thy pictures be,
> Much pleasure, then from thee much more must flow,
> And soonest our best men with thee do go.
> Rest of their bones, and soul's delivery.
> Thou art slave to fate, chance, kings, and desperate men,
> And dost with poison, war, and sickness dwell.
> And poppy or charms can make us sleep as well,
> And better than thy stroke: Why swell'st thou then?
> One short sleep past, we wake eternally.
> And death shall be no more; death thou shalt die.

One has a choice to make in this life. Will death have the last word, or will Jesus Christ, the Word? Will Christ lead us through death to life again and forever? Death may come to us at any time. We do not know what will happen to us tomorrow. But Jesus Christ can come to us now to give us the faith that swallows up death. I urge you to choose life and its Lord.

Paul, at the close of his life, was able to say, "For I am already on the point of being sacrificed: the time of my departure has come. I have fought the good fight. I have finished the race. I have kept the faith. Henceforth, there is laid up for me the crown of righteousness, which the Lord, the righteous judge, will award to me on that day. And not only to me but also to all who have loved his appearing." May this be our approach as well as we prepare to go into God's presence shouting "God's yes to life is louder than death's no."

Amen

For Study and Meditation

"'To Err Is Human, to Forgive . . .'"
(Matthew 18:21-35; Romans 4:1-8)

♦ Silence is not easy to come by in our busy lives. It is difficult, even for the most spiritually disciplined people! It is especially useful, though, in centering the heart. Seek silence to center your heart on God's grace and forgiveness. It is significant to note that the same letters in *silent* are in the word *listen*. Take time to *listen* to all that God longs to say to you in your time of silence.

♦ Confess to God the unforgiveness in your heart. Ask him to release you from any bitterness and resentment you may be carrying. Commit to pray for these people daily. Take time to ask who you might have wronged. Ask God for the strength to make amends with those people.

♦ Fast for 24 hours from food or something else (perhaps television, music, telephone use). Fasting, more than any other discipline, will reveal to you what binds you. Use this time of fasting to reflect on evidences of God's grace in your own life and the lives of the people around you. Keep a journal close to record and reflect.

THOUGHTS FOR FURTHER REFLECTION

"Forgiveness is not a mere option for a Christian; it is an obligation."

Ben Witherington III

"To you the good news needs to be told that forgiveness is not about one's worthiness to receive it but rather the graciousness and worth of the one who gives it."

Ben Witherington III

"There is nothing that makes us love someone so much as praying for them."

William Law

"O merciful God, fill our hearts, we pray you, with the graces of your Holy Spirit, with love, joy, peace, long-suffering, gentleness, goodness, faith, meekness, temperance. Teach us to love those who hate us; to pray for those who despitefully use us; that we may be your children, our Father, who makes your sun to shine on the evil and on the good and sends rain on the just and on the unjust."

St. Anselm

"Eternal Treasures in Earthen Vessels"
(2 Corinthians 4:7-18)

- Meditate on 2 Corinthians 4:7-18. This is a powerful passage about God's power to sustain us in our sufferings, especially when we consider the plight of Paul. At the writing of this letter to the Corinthians, his body was probably covered with welts and scars from the terrible beatings he had received. He was physically at a breaking point. For all intents and purposes, his life was a nightmare. But through it all he managed to give praise and glory to God. For Paul, these hardships do not show what humans are made of but what God's power looks like. How has God revealed himself to you (and through you!) in your sufferings?
- Memorize 2 Corinthians 4:16-18 over the next few days. These verses are a radiant reminder that though we will encounter suffering, God has already overcome this world. He can and will sustain us in all our trials and sufferings.
- Serve another person you know who is suffering. Pray about how God

might use you to be a living expression of 2 Corinthians 4:7-18 for another.

THOUGHTS FOR FURTHER REFLECTION

"When life throws you a curveball, will you recognize it and swing away, or will you complain it's an unfair pitch?"

Ben Witherington III

"Only by dying could Jesus rise to new resurrection life that was far better and more powerful than the life he had before. So it is, and so it shall be for us as well."

Ben Witherington III

"God does not give us overcoming life; He gives us life as we overcome."

Oswald Chambers

"God does not lead his children around hardship, but leads them straight through it. But he leads! And amidst the hardship, he is nearer to them than ever before."

Otto Dibelius

"Grounds for Differences"
(Ezekiel 17:1-10, 22-24; Mark 4:1-20)

♦ Study Ezekiel 17:22-24. Read through the passage several times slowly, reflecting on the beautiful imagery found here. Take note of what God is promising in this passage. The Lord aims to make of us something big!
♦ Meditate on the Bible passages and on the sermon you just read. Take time to journal about what you sense God is asking you to do for the

sake of his Kingdom. Determine to take the necessary next steps in obedience to his call.

* Pray for wisdom and guidance in your daily walk. Pray for opportunities to do the work God has called you to do. Ask God to guide you and sustain you as you seek to do his will.

Thoughts for Further Reflection

"The Kingdom of God is at hand. There is work to be done. There will be failures and successes. But the work shall bear fruit."

Ben Witherington III, paraphrasing Mark 4:1-20

"To God there is nothing small. The moment we have given it to God, it becomes infinite."

Mother Teresa

"O God, be all my love, all my hope, all my striving; let my thoughts and words flow from you, my daily life be in you, and every breath I take be for you."

John Cassian

"Death Be Not Proud"
(Philippians 1:12-26; 1 Corinthians 15:54-58; 1 Timothy 4:6-8)

* Pray through the words of "Take My Life," an old hymn written by Frances Havergal in 1874, and worship God as you read or sing through the words of this beautiful song.

Take my life, and let it be consecrated, Lord, to Thee.
Take my moments and my days; let them flow in ceaseless praise.
Take my hands, and let them move at the impulse of Thy love.
Take my feet, and let them be swift and beautiful for Thee.
Take my voice, and let me sing always, only, for my King.

Take my lips, and let them be filled with messages from Thee.
Take my silver and my gold; not a mite would I withhold.
Take my intellect, and use every power as Thou shalt choose.
Take my will, and make it Thine; it shall be no longer mine.
Take my heart, it is Thine own; it shall be Thy royal throne.
Take my love, my Lord, I pour at Thy feet its treasure store.
Take myself, and I will be ever, only, all for Thee.

THOUGHTS FOR FURTHER REFLECTION

"Let us thank God for giving us the victory through our Lord Jesus Christ. Never give in and never admit defeat. Keep on working at the Lord's work always. Know that in the Lord you cannot be laboring in vain."

Ben Witherington III

"Alive, I'm Christ's messenger; dead, I'm his bounty. Life versus even more life! I can't lose."

Philippians 1:21, *The Message*

"Dearest Lord, teach me to be generous; teach me to serve thee as thou deservest; to give and not to count the cost, to fight and not to heed the wounds, to toil and not to seek for rest, to labor and not to seek reward, save that of knowing that I do thy will."

St. Ignatius of Loyola (1491-1556)

HOLY WEEK AND EASTERTIDE

The Light Rises

Fool's Goal

Psalm 14 and Luke 16:19-31

The Disease of Disbelief

Atheism is a strange disease of the human soul and it takes many forms —
actual and deliberate unbelief, disbelief, or what I prefer to call practical
atheism, by which I mean persons who live as though there is no God and
no consequences to their actions, regardless of what they profess to believe. To be sure, there is enough suffering and evil in this world to lead one
to doubt the existence of a good God. But only a few persons have had the
guts or foolhardiness to state flatly, "There is no God," as the fool does in
Psalm 14. But notice even here the fool says this "in his heart," not in public
where he might be criticized for such a statement. Not too many people
will simply say this in public. One famous exception was, of course, the
philosopher Friedrich Nietzsche who publicly stated, "God is dead." Perhaps more recently you have seen one of the many billboards with Nietzsche's famous claim, under which is printed, "'Nietzsche is dead' — God."
Most human beings realize we do not have exhaustive knowledge of reality
and cannot categorically rule God out of existence.

This fact is probably one main reason our psalmist calls such a person as Nietzsche a fool. Now a fool, a character who shows up regularly in
Proverbs and also in the Psalms and other forms of wisdom literature, is
not a person who is an ignoramus, or a simpleton, or an unintelligent person. A fool, rather, is a rash, impudent, imprudent, arrogant person. Recently I debated on national television with the president of the American
Skeptics Society. He was an interesting and intelligent man, but what one

immediately noticed about the man is that he "protested too much." He was trying extremely hard to discredit God and Jesus and their significance. But if God does not exist, why the incessant need to deny God exists? Could it be that deep inside the person really suspects God does exist but simply does not like the idea because it requires accepting that one is not the master of one's own fate and the captain of one's own soul? I suspect this is often at the bottom of all the protest. Creatures created in God's image will always hear the whispering inside, even in their innermost being, that God exists. Atheism is a self-defeating disease, which frustrates its victims and beguiles them into believing they are in control of their own lives.

Practical Atheism

Perhaps more characteristic are those who have known God or known about God but have fallen away from that knowledge and the relationship it involved. Jean-Paul Sartre, the famous existentialist philosopher, once wrote in his autobiography, "I have just related the story of a missed vocation. I needed God, he was given to me, he vegetated in me for a while and then died. Whenever anyone speaks to me today about him, I say, with the amusement of an old beau who meets a former belle — 'Fifty years ago, had it not been for a misunderstanding, that mistake, that accident which separated us, there might have been something between us.'"

We encounter ever so many people like this every day — former churchgoers, children of Christian parents who have wandered away from church, people who have had their feelings hurt in church and never returned, people who think God abandoned them in a crisis or an hour of need, people who have burned out or have been burned by too much, too fast, too soon, or too long. Yet even practical atheists suspect there is a God, and since they are not in right relationship with God, they sometimes worry about their eternal status.

The managing editor of Havana's daily newspaper was once interviewed openly by western reporters and he defended the communist system and said that he had to renounce his previous participation in the church to join the Communist Party there and stressed that the communist system had been good for Cuba overall. But when the cameras stopped rolling and the editor was away from his bugged office he told them: "I was a Christian but I threw in my lot with Castro. The revolution has been good for Cuba, I believe . . . but please pray for me, just in case there is a God." One of the clearest signs of a practical atheist with a bad conscience is a request for prayer. Someone once defined a hypocrite as a person who writes a book on atheism and then prays that it sells. It is also interesting how many people, when they get in a desperate situation, will begin instinctively to call upon God for help, even when the only way God has ever passed their lips before was in an oath or curse of some kind. Could it be that even practical atheists find atheism impractical from time to time? Can they really be sure that there is nothing beyond the grave? The answer to this question is, of course, No — no human being has ever known for sure that there is no afterlife, much less that there is no God.

The Rich Man and Lazarus

Sometimes life plays very strange tricks on us. The story is told of two pastors named Jones in the same Pennsylvania town. One Rev. Jones himself passed away while on vacation in Florida with friends. The other Rev. Jones lost his wife during the course of the same week while also on vacation, only he was with his wife at the time. Early the next week the former Rev. Jones's wife received a postcard from Florida from her now-deceased husband which read, "Really missing you. The heat here is awful." During that same week a postcard came to the latter Rev. Jones's district superintendent which read, "My wife has passed away, please send a substitute for the weekend."

It is that kind of shocking and surprising turn of events that we have related in the parable of the rich person and Lazarus. The story has already been read to us this morning and so there are simply a few points worth stressing. The rich man, who trusted in his own wealth and prosperity, died, and none of his vast resources could prevent such an outcome. All human beings living in a fallen world are terminal, and it is only a fool, not a wise person, who does not live keeping this fact steadily in view. The most doctors and medicines can do is delay the inevitable. Unfortunately, for the rich person in the parable, the shock of recognition does not come until the afterlife, when he wakes up in Hades, clamoring for a drink of water, but too late. His was a life much like many practical atheists who discover only too late the consequences of such a self-centered, rather than

God-centered, life. This parable is meant to be a wake-up call, reminding its audience that one needs to make things right with God in this lifetime, for it will be too late once one dies. The rich fool's destination is fire, according to this parable, inextinguishable fire, however unfashionable it may be to say so in our age. One of the most ironic notes in this text for Holy Week is that Jesus says flatly that if people won't believe the Word of God (in this case Moses' version of it) they also won't believe the work of God — someone coming back from the dead to warn them. The problem lies not in the lack of Word or work of God, but in the disbelieving heart.

On the other hand we have Lazarus, the poor diseased man who is set forward as an example of godly piety, and who ends up reclining at table with Abraham in heaven! But how in the world can Lazarus be an example of piety? Isn't he just a diseased beggar in the parable who dies? Do we really know anything about his piety?

Actually, the answer is Yes, if we have paid close attention to Luke's Gospel as a whole and to the many passages that lead up to this parable. For one thing we have already heard the beatitude of Jesus — "Blessed are you who are poor, for yours is the Dominion of God" (6:20). Another way one could render this verse would be, "Blessed are those who know they are needy (and trust God), for he will take care of them."

You might never have thought of this, but being in want, being needy, is often a sure cure for practical atheism. A poor person knows that he or she cannot make it alone. Poor people know they need outside help. Daily they are forced to scrounge and beg to survive. When you are in exigent circumstances, praying comes regularly to mind. This is why during World War I it came to be said that "there are no atheists in foxholes." When you are facing your mortality daily due to danger or disease or poverty there is little danger that you will see yourself as godlike or self-sufficent. And so in Luke's Gospel the poor are often depicted as pious, and of course the outcome of the parable makes clear just how pious this man was. Angels conveyed him directly to the bosom of Abraham! Blessed are those who know their need for God. If ever we wanted a story that disproved the American myth that wealth is a necessary sign that one has been blessed by God, and poverty a sure sign of lack of faith, this is the story. And all of this raises important questions for you and me.

What Kind of Fool Do You Think I Am?

"What kind of fool am I?" Have you ever asked yourself this question? Are you like the fool in Psalm 14 who secretly denies God in his heart, but publicly appears and pretends to be pious? Or are you like the fool who publicly denies the existence of God, even though he knows he does not have an exhaustive knowledge of reality and the space-time continuum? Or perhaps are you like the hedonistic fool in Jesus' parable, all caught up in the lifestyle of conspicuous consumption and ignoring death's calling card, even when it stands at the door? Or are you foolish enough to really believe in God, but not to wholeheartedly trust him? Are you like Peter, walking two steps on the water and then sinking when fear wins out over faith?

Or, on the other hand, are you a holy fool, who knows that the foolishness of God is wiser than the wisdom of all human beings? Do you know, as the Apostle Paul says in 1 Corinthians 1, that God chose the death of his Son as the means to give us life, and the foolishness of preaching this message as the means of our salvation? In the end, it is not a question of whether we will be fools — all humans are foolish in one way or another. The question is whether we are foolish enough to believe Jesus when he says "whosoever believes on him shall not perish but have everlasting life." For that is the holy fool's goal, and it is not in the end fool's gold at all.

Amen

Sincere — Sin's Here

2 Samuel 11:2-27 and 12:1-7; Psalm 51

The Extent of Sin

Sin, say the scholars, is a religious concept. Before one believes one has sinned, one must first believe that there is someone, namely God, that one is sinning against. If there are no divinely sanctioned, universal rights and wrongs in this world, then we are free to set up our own standards. In short, everyone can do what is right in his or her own eyes. The loss of the sense of sin in the modern era is an inevitable result of the loss of a belief and trust in God. And this loss is a frightening one. As Thomas Carlyle said, "The deadliest sin is the consciousness of no sin." There are so many people in the world today who have so lost their way that even their conscience is anesthetized. They have no remorse about stealing, lying, killing. Their motto is, "Might makes right." Or, "I'll do it my way." Yet even those guilty of a lifelong pattern of crime and sin are not beyond the grasp of God's grace. The Good News in Psalm 51 is that even an old murderer and adulterer like King David can receive God's mercy.

First, we need to understand the extent and nature of sin. If we do not see the extent of our sin, we will not see the extent of our need for God and his grace. When I was in England I had an occasion to sit in the pews during a service which involved a time when people were urged to come forward to the front and pray prayers of confession. As the man in front of me rose to go forward and pray, his wife tugged on his suit coat and said in a whisper, "Sit down, Henry, you haven't sinned!" Obviously one won't think there's a need for confession if one doesn't see they have sinned or are a sinner. In the normal course of things, the more superficial one's view of sin, the more superficial one's view of our need for God and grace.

It is characteristic of human beings that they are frequently blind to their own faults and besetting sins. You can see pride and arrogance and jealousy and lust and selfishness in others, but not in yourself. Thomas Nast, the well-known cartoonist, was on one occasion present with other guests at a party. He drew a caricature of everyone present and then passed them around for all to see. The result was quite interesting. Everyone present recognized the caricature of every other person and enjoyed a hearty laugh. But there was a large group who could not recognize their own pictures. So it is with us. Everyone has his or her blind spot. We fail to see ourselves as we really are.

Perhaps this blindness is in part caused by the fact that we are too close to and too much enamored of the subject at hand, that is, ourselves. It is hard to get an objective view when we are both the subject and object of the investigation. We are rather like a person who looks at a large painting from an inch away. We don't see the pattern or the overall impression. Even King David did not fully see the error of his ways until Nathan came and pointed it out to him.

Psalm 51 makes perfectly clear to us that we are not only sinners in our deeds and by our choices, we are also sinners by nature. Not only is every human being since Adam and Eve born into a world of sin, but there is also the fact that we inherit a sinful nature from them. We are born with a tendency toward selfishness and self-centeredness, toward rebellion against authority and rules. We are born with a nature that whispers to us, "Go ahead and sin; don't resist temptation, indulge in it." Oscar Wilde, the poet and playwright, once remarked, "I can resist anything but temptation." There is more truth than humor in this.

A person outside of Christ is in bondage to his or her sinful nature and tendencies. The psalmist puts it this way — "I was brought forth in iniquity." This does not mean that marital relations are sinful, or that the act of bearing a child is sinful, but that from conception sin is part of our makeup. We cannot escape it. We can only inherit it. Perhaps now you can see the reason why Jesus was not conceived by the normal means. Only by a virginal conception, only by God overshadowing Mary and giving her a son, could Jesus avoid inheriting our sinful nature.

If our deeds were the only thing that was sinful about us, God would not have had to give us a new nature in Christ. It is because we have a disease of the human heart called sin-sickness, not just because we have done sick deeds, that we need a new heart, and need to be made new creatures. Doubtless, we are not as bad as we could be. But when we look around us at all the violence, war, poverty, persecution, and oppression, this certifies loud and clear the existence of our sinful natures. And if we think we are not guilty or responsible for these situations, then we deceive ourselves, because we bury our heads in the sand and do nothing to correct these injustices. We are thereby guilty of a monumental sin of omission. Thus, we can all say of ourselves not just, "I have sinned," but also, "I am a sinner by nature and also by choice." Why? Because we willingly indulge that nature. But we have not passed the point of no return.

Giving Up the Sin — Confession Is Good for the Soul

Changing human behavior is not easy. We are so used to behaving in a certain way that we have gotten to the point where our vices have become habits, even habits we enjoy. Sometimes we willingly listen to the preacher tell us to flee sin: we flee — but we leave a forwarding address. There is a story about a mother of eight. She had been visiting next door and when she went back home and came in the front door, there were her children all huddled in the center of the floor on her new carpet very much involved with something wiggly and squirmy. On closer inspection, and to her total dismay, she discovered her children were playing with a family of baby skunks. In her horror she screamed, "Children, skunks, run!" at which point each child picked up a skunk and ran! You cannot run from your own nature; you take it with you wherever you go. As Shakespeare once said, "Be sure your sins will find you out," as David discovered in the celebrated Bathsheba affair.

When we encounter David in Psalm 51, fortunately he has gotten to the point where he is sick of his sickness — his sin sickness — and is ready to swallow the medicine. The beginning of the healing comes with confession. David says he is painfully aware of his sin and its extent, and in fact it is constantly on his mind and he needs help to deal with. He is also aware that every sin is an affront to God, a sin against God. In fact, at one juncture he even says, "Against you alone have I sinned. . . ."

David realizes he has been living a lie, despite the fact that as king he is supposed to be a moral example to his people. David owns his sin, and he does not try to justify it; rather, he simply confesses it in all its horror. He realizes that confession simply opens us up to God, like opening a festering wound. Confession itself is not the cure nor the cleansing — God provides that. Furthermore, forgiveness is not all that is required, because if there is just forgiveness then there is no changed nature. Actually, cleansing and change are required, not merely pardoning. In fact, a whole new perspective on life is also required.

Picture Martin Luther as an Augustinian monk in Germany in 1511. He would go to confession, sometimes for up to six hours at a time, in order to share with God every slight flaw in his character and behavior. He literally believed that every iota of sin had to be confessed in order to be forgiven. He found no real remedy in all this confessing, any more than he did in a string of good works, or in a barrage of good advice from various mentors. Eventually he realized it was not enough to feel sorry for wrongdoings or even to confess them all — he needed a new nature, a fresh start. He needed to say with our psalmist, "Create in me a clean heart, O God."

It is interesting that in Psalm 51 David thinks of his sin as like leprosy, and so he talks about hyssop purging him. Hyssop comes from the caper plant and was used in the rituals of purification for lepers and those defiled by touching corpses. David is in essence saying, "Because of my sin I am an outcast to society and cast out by God, cut off from fellowship with both." Thus he prays for cleansing so that those broken relationships can be renewed and restarted. But God has made clear to him the weight and gravity of his sin, so David cries out, "Let the bones which thou hast crushed rejoice."

New Creatures, Not Just Nice Guys

David has asked for the return of the joy of his salvation, the joy of knowing and experiencing the cleansing of God. He says, in essence, "Clean me out, then fill me up with your Spirit." But he also asks for a more steadfast human spirit. Cleansing and strengthening of the inner self are required, not just the gift of the Spirit. In fact, David pleads, "Take not your Holy Spirit from me." This reminds us that it is indeed possible to quench the Spirit and its work in one's life. The horror of apostasy — the active, willful rebellion against God persisted in and insisted on — is that it is possible to blaspheme that Spirit within your life. It is possible that the Spirit may depart the temple of your body. Thus David pleads, "Let it not be so in my case." David knew that he had departed and was apart from God because of his sin, but he did not want God to depart from him.

Like so many sinners before and after him, David makes some bold promises that if God will just reshape him, he will testify of God's work in his life and thereby show other transgressors that if God can redeem even an old murderer and adulterer like David, he can redeem anyone. The good news is that drastic change can happen in a person's life, change for the better. Graham Kerr was the Galloping Gourmet of television and cookbook fame in the 1970s, a millionaire success story. But in 1975 he and his wife were in a near-fatal car crash, and his wife had a nervous breakdown. Humbled, brought to his knees, Kerr was converted to Christianity and sold most of his possessions. Yet he continued his profession, working wholeheartedly to relieve the problems of world hunger instead of promoting the sin of gluttony, one of our nation's real besetting sins.

The God who heard and helped King David become a new person is also the God who transformed Graham Kerr in our own era, and indeed can transform any sinner. To be sure, what God is looking for is not merely nice persons, but new creatures transformed by his grace. He calls out to all of us, "Sinner why do you persist in this path? Do you not know it leads to your own destruction? But I am God and not a human being — so turn and live and be transformed into the divine likeness, and I will restore unto you a joy, a joy of living and loving and salvation that will eclipse anything you have ever known before. Though your sins be as scarlet, I will wash them white as snow." Or, to put it colloquially, though your sins be as bad as David's — it is not too late to turn and live.

Amen

The Temptations of God

Matthew 4:1-11; Luke 4:1-13

Maundy Thursday

Desert Days

They were out there in the desert a very long time. The Scripture says forty years. They wandered and wandered and wandered. There was a whiff of escape when the spies came back and reported on the land oozing with milk and honey, but they were afraid and intimidated. They saw themselves like grasshoppers standing next to giants. Manna (which literally means "what is it?") showed up with regularity and they ate, but they still grumbled and complained about leftovers. Pheasant or quail showed up as well, which suited a low-carb diet, but these folks were not partial to meat. And so they complained, bitterly. They murmured to Moses and behind his back. And they disobeyed God's explicit commands, the words now enshrined in the Pentateuch. They worshiped a golden calf while Moses was on sabbatical at Sinai. And they failed the test. Only two of them ever entered the Promised Land, and Moses wasn't one of those two.

There was another Jew who wandered out into the chalk wilderness we would call desert. He didn't take any food with him, and when you fast for as long as he did, you can see a lot of things out there in the unrelenting heat. But perhaps I do not need to tell you this. Perhaps you've already been there. This fellow went out there where it was too hot to even sweat anymore and he didn't eat. Now when you don't eat for that long a lot of things start looking good — even bread-shaped stones. And, yes, he was tempted to break his fast, but he didn't while he was out there forty days

95

alone. This fellow says he met the Devil out there and he tested his mettle, and I believe him. The desert's no place to be alone.

The Temptations of God

Temptation frames the ministry of Jesus. In Matthew 4 we hear of the temptation to change the character of his ministry, while in Gethsemane we hear of the temptation to change the conclusion of his ministry. Both come to him at a time of extreme stress and testing and, humanly speaking, of weakness. Jesus may have gone from the wilderness to the garden, but in both these venues the saying from the garden applies — "The human spirit is willing, but the flesh is weak" (or as one fumbling translator once rendered the Greek, "The ghost is ready, but the meat is soft"). But then, isn't it usually at times of extreme lows or highs that temptations press in upon us? Stressful times when we are tempted to go off-roading?

Notice from our Luke 4 text this evening that we are told that while empty of belly Jesus was full of the Spirit. Oddly enough, at our spiritually highest moments, even visionary moments, we can be at our most vulnerable to temptation. The lesson, I suppose, is that if one is going to go off into the desert alone, especially into that kind of desert, there are two things one must not leave home without — the Holy Spirit and the Holy Word. Had Jesus not been full of the Holy Spirit, had he been relying simply on his human spirit, he might not have endured the temptations that bookend his earthly ministry. Likewise, if he was not full of the Word, he would not have endured either. We need to come fully to grips with the fact that Jesus was temptable. The author of Hebrews reminds us that he was tested like us in every regard, but without sin. It was not impossible for him to commit sin. Had it been impossible for him to do that, it would not have been possible for him to commit virtue either, if we can put it that way.

Notice that in the desert the temptation begins by appealing to the point at which Jesus was most viscerally vulnerable — he was hungry. Indeed, he was so hungry that when Satan urged him to turn stones into bread, even the stones began to look good to him. He was being asked to put his personal need over the commitment he had made to fast and undergo his own personal wilderness wandering. Of course, the underlying temptation was to obey Satan rather than God, and in fact one could say that any temptation has as its subplot the question of whether we will choose God or Satan, the question of whom we will choose to serve in both little and large matters. As Bob Dylan said in his classic song, "You gotta serve somebody. It might be the Devil or it might be the Lord, but you gotta serve somebody." Though humans love to be served, in fact that was not what they were made for — they were made to serve another and they will do so whether willingly or unwillingly, whether wittingly or unwittingly.

In the second temptation in Luke (it is the third in Matthew), Satan offers all authority and splendor over kingdoms if Jesus will worship him. The greatest of human temptations is always to worship something as God (whether it be self, some other creature, some creative force, some part of nature) that is less than and other than God. Temptation, of course, always comes with great promise of benefits or rewards if one will just succumb to the temptation. When we hear that Jesus was tempted, we must realize this means that on occasion he was inclined to do what was not God's will for his life. This is made clear in Gethsemane when Jesus says, "Nevertheless not my will but yours be done." Were he not so inclined, had he not been allured to some degree, one could not really say that his temptations had been tempting. But the good news for all of us is that it is one thing to be tempted, another thing to sin. Notice that Jesus does not dispute that Satan has these kingdoms to dispense. Indeed, elsewhere he calls him "the ruler of this world," though he adds that he has been judged.

The third temptation in Luke entails a gratuitous use of power by Jesus to demonstrate his identity to Israel. Yet the real temptation here was to put God to the test, to try and force God to use his great power to deliver Jesus from calamity and great harm. But to test God is the very opposite of to trust God. Jesus had to resist the temptation to test God by making a spectacle of himself, trying to draw attention to himself.

But what is God's role in all of this adventure or misadventure? Does God tempt Jesus? Why do we pray, to God no less, "lead us not into temptation"? Perhaps we may say that God tests us, as he tested Job, but the intent of the test is to strengthen our character, whereas the Devil tempts us intending to destroy our character. And here is the mystery — the very same event in Job's life or Jesus' can be both test and temptation. God allowed Job and Jesus to be stretched by the Devil. But the Devil and God had differing aims in the event. Notice that we are told in the Markan allusion to the temptation scene (Mark 1:12) that it was God's Spirit who thrust Jesus out into the wilderness.

Man and Manna in the Wilderness

What were Jesus' resources in the wilderness and in the garden for resisting temptation? In each instance in the wilderness Jesus replies to Satan by quoting from the Pentateuch. He seems especially partial to Deuteronomy at this juncture, which I doubt would have been the book that first leapt to my mind had I been in his tight spot. What we notice is that Jesus puts himself under the authority of God's Word here, or to put it another way, he draws on the same resources we have to resist temptation — the Word of God and the Spirit of God. Jesus was a man under authority and so he was not free to do as he pleased, or even as he was tempted to do if he was to be the true Son of God, and also the true Son of Man.

As has often been noted, the Devil is equally capable of quoting Scripture for his own ends. The mere ability to quote Scripture, even quote it accurately, is no guarantee that one will endure and prevail over temptation. It is, rather, *how* one responds and submits to the Word and whether one will rely on the Spirit that will determine whether one successfully passes the test. And indeed passing the test is possible even for us. Paul puts it this way in 1 Corinthians 10: "No trial [or test] has overcome you that is not common to humanity such that with the temptation [or test] God will provide an adequate means of escape."

Put another way, one can say that the Word without the Spirit provides no adequate defense against temptation, for then we have no power or strength to endure. But the Spirit without the Word leaves us with no concrete answer to temptation, and it too is inadequate. Notice how in Luke the text says that after Jesus passed the threefold test Satan left him "until an opportune time." This was only the beginning of the struggle for Jesus, and any time anyone attempts something great for God, there will be such temptations and struggles. We see the sequel to this struggle in Gethsemane.

The Testing and the Character of Christ

Tonight and tomorrow especially we need to know "in whom we have believed." We need to know the character of the Christ, our Savior. So let us briefly review. What were the great temptations of Jesus? To place the satisfaction of a personal need or desire over the fulfillment of a commitment made to God. To take shortcuts to achieve the desired ends of ministry. Jesus was expecting to become ruler of the nations, but not by first worshiping Satan and short-circuiting the path God would have him tread. Rather, he was to be the one who stooped to conquer, who went to the Cross so he might be lifted up as Lord, and might light us up as well. He was also tempted to take dramatic and desperate measures to prove to his hard-to-convince audience that he was indeed the Christ. Finally he was tempted to bypass the Cross itself.

What does all of this tell us about Jesus? Of course it tells us that he was fully human and could be tempted, but it tells us much more as well. It also tells us, paradoxically enough, that he was the divine Son of God, for only such a person could and would have these precise temptations. Now of course, some who have been insane megalomaniacs may have been deluded into thinking they have had such temptations, but Jesus, by all accounts, was quite sane and sanguine about what was and was not the case, including what was the case when it came to his own identity.

So I say again: these are the temptations that only the divine Son of God could and must face, though we may learn much from them about the more mundane temptations we face daily. Put bluntly, Jesus' greatest temptation was to "push the God button" — or in Gethsemane to have God push it for him — and change the divine design for his life. His great temptation, unlike ours, was not primarily to act in a more fallibly human way but to act in a divine way that would in fact obliterate his true humanity. His great temptation was to so use the divine power, knowledge, character he had that he ceased to submit to the limitations of time, space, knowledge, and power that humans all face. And in his great hymnic passage in Philippians 2:5-11 Paul tells us that it was the very nature of the Incarnation that Jesus stripped himself of his divine prerogatives in order to take on human form and be a servant amongst humankind.

Think about it for a moment. I have known plenty of bad cooks who could turn bread into stones, but I have not really met ones who were tempted to turn stones into bread. And yet this was a real temptation for Jesus. I have also not met any truly sane and normal Christian humans who were tempted to throw themselves off the Sears Tower in Chicago just to give God the chance to rescue them, much less to prove their own divinity! And of course in Gethsemane Jesus' desire to bypass the Cross has nothing to do with a mere reluctance to die. He speaks of letting the cup of God's wrath poured out on sin bypass him. In other words, he is tempted to bypass becoming the atoning sacrifice for the sins of the world since it means facing God's wrath against sin on the Cross. It means embracing our godforsakenness, when previously in life he had only known intimacy with his Abba. This is no normal human temptation. No one else could really be inclined to turn down being the Savior of the world when he knew in fact he had it in himself to be the One. You see, Jesus' great temptation in the desert was to so draw on the divine power or knowledge he had access to that he would cease to be the Son of Man, for he would be drawing on resources we do not have because we do not have divine natures, unlike the Christ. Had he done this he could no longer have been our exemplar. His great temptation in the garden was to save himself and so doom us all to remaining lost. Paradoxically enough, the one person for whom Jesus did not need to die — himself — is the one person who had to die if sinners were to be reconciled to God. For only he had passed the temptations test.

So here is where I tell you that the power and knowledge and abilities Jesus manifested during his ministry and bequeathed to his disciples are those he received from the full endowment of the Holy Spirit, an endowment available to all of us, and the knowledge of the Word of God, a knowledge available to all of us. By the power of the Spirit and the power of the Word Jesus both fended off temptation and even performed his miracles, the very same resources we have. Jesus' temptation was to act as God and so cease to be fully human, but he chose to respond as fully human and use only the resources we have to resist temptation or take up the tasks of ministry.

WWJD?

When I was young and in Sunday school, it used to bother me when the teacher would say, "Be like Jesus." To my mind, that was quite impossible, precisely because Jesus had a "God button" to get him out of tight scrapes, and I did not. It was pointless asking, "What would Jesus do?" since I didn't have the nature or resources to emulate him. But then I learned that Jesus had humbled himself and used only the resources we have at hand to overcome temptation and do the will of God. And so it is true that his example truly stands in Scripture for us to follow.

We may say, on a lesser scale, that we too have been tempted to break a commitment to satisfy a personal desire or need which has been legitimate — to choose a personal good over what was best in the situation. Jesus did not, however, perform gratuitous miracles during his ministry for his own benefit or even to enhance his reputation; they were always acts of compassion or revelation. We surely have also all faced the temptation to take shortcuts, to use any means necessary to accomplish laudable ends. Furthermore, we have faced the temptation to seek a quick fix, to seek our own fame and glory, to seek to force God's hand by making a spectacle of ourselves and so put God to the test. Life is the proving ground of discipleship and I guarantee you that the temptations we face now will come back to haunt us later if we do not resist them repeatedly and vigorously. Satan is looking for an opportune time to sift us again, but Jesus in the garden and in heaven has prayed for us that we might turn, and help others to turn round as well.

There was a man who went out into the desert alone . . . but then, you probably know this story. You've been there before yourself.

Amen

The Sorrow of God

Isaiah 53:1-12

Good Friday

As I Lay Dying

The corporal lay on the battlefield bleeding to death. He screamed out for a medic. Despite a flurry of crossfire, the medic, who was also the army chaplain, managed to crawl over to the young man and gave him morphine to kill the pain. As the boy lay there dying he looked into the medic's eyes and said, "Chaplain, what is God like? Surely you know." What can you say to a question like this when all you can see in all directions is blood and death? What can you tell a young man in the midst of a senseless tragedy or a painful death? The scene I just described was a real one that took place on a South Pacific island in World War II. The medic was my college Bible professor and mentor at Carolina, Dr. Bernard Boyd. He said in relating this scene, and I agree with him, that the only answer that meaningfully addresses this question has to do with the paradox of Good Friday, the paradox of a loving but suffering God, who in the person of his Son died on the Cross for you and me.

Cross Talk

What, then, does the Cross actually tell us about God and the human dilemma and how the former relates to the latter? Surely it tells us in the first place that God is holy, just, and fair. On the one hand it shows us how hideous sin is in the eyes of God. Let us be frank — it is our sin, the sin of all

102

humanity, which necessitated Jesus' death on the Cross, and in his dying he bore the punishment for that sin in our place. The Cross tells us that for us to have fellowship with God, considering God's holiness and our sinfulness, something had to be done about our fallen condition.

We live today in a world that would like to be a no-fault world — no-fault divorce, no-fault car accidents, no-fault deaths, and so on. But that is not the world that God created. In God's world it's always a matter of truth or consequences. Since God could not forsake his holy nature and we could not redeem ourselves, no matter how many self improvement programs we might undertake, something had to be done about the sin problem or else our relationship with God would always be a broken one. As the Bible says, God cannot forever overlook or ignore sin. Eventually the problem has to be dealt with. A price had to be paid. Whatever your concept of God, if it is the biblical God we are referring to, it cannot involve God's not caring about justice, fairness, righteousness, or holiness. It cannot involve a definition of love, or even Love Incarnate, that ignores these traits and concerns of God. Let me put it to you this way: if you think it is easy for God to forgive sin, take a good, hard look at the Cross.

That which we wear around our necks as jewelry was actually the ancient Roman equivalent of the electric chair. The death of Jesus on the Cross would be a pointless, brutal tragedy if we could not see it in the light of its sequel — the Resurrection of Jesus. Forgiving sin cost God the life of his only begotten Child. There can be no higher price to pay. Which one of us would give up the life of even one of our children to save even one other human being's life? Not many of us, I'd wager.

And let it be said here that if Jesus' death on the Cross was not the one absolutely necessary and sufficient means of our salvation, then God the Father is in no sense a loving God. What sort of God would require that of his own Son, if it was not absolutely necessary to atone for our sins? But, paradoxically, if it was the necessary and sufficient means of atonement, then it becomes the greatest expression on earth of God's love for us.

The Jews had a saying that they applied to crucifixion, even though it was originally about the displaying of someone's corpse on a tree to shame him and his family. The saying is, "Cursed be he who hangs upon a tree" (Deut. 21:23). They did not look on crucifixion as in any way a noble or honorable way to die. They saw it as shameful and as a sign that God had cursed the person in question. How could one possibly talk about a crucified Messiah? That was as much an oxymoron, or contradiction in terms, for early Jews as talking about a good Samaritan. Jews, so far as we can tell, basically did not read the story in Isaiah 53, our text for today, to apply to the Messiah. They saw the Messiah as the Anointed One of God who would triumph over Israel's foes, not die a shameful death at their hands. One must keep in mind as well that ancient peoples believed that how one died most revealed that person's character. No Jews in their right mind would have made up a story about a crucified Messiah. It's too improbable *not* to be true. That Jesus died on the Cross was a sign to most that he was a weak, powerless, wicked person, for he was dying a death reserved for the extreme criminal element — those who were revolutionaries or committed treason. In a sense, of course, they were right about Jesus being judged by God — it's just that he was being judged in our place.

For the Holy Love of God

God, however, thankfully, is not just a holy God. God is a God of holy love, and we should stress the noun a bit more than the adjective. It was not just that God was just when he sent Jesus to die, for, as John 3:16 puts it, "God so loved the world that he sent his only begotten Son. . . ." By sending his Son to die in our place he was able to express his holy love — not just holiness without love, and not love without holiness. Some time ago there was a movie entitled *Love Story,* which had as its theme, "Love means never having to say you're sorry." It was a no-fault definition of love — indeed, one could say it was one of the sorriest definitions of love ever. Real love, costly love, means always that we must ask for forgiveness from those whom we love when we have wronged them. There can be no real love without forgiveness and reconciliation in a world full of alienation and dysfunctional relationships both between God and us and between human beings. Real love, as 1 Corinthians 13 puts it, is patient, kind, self-sacrificial, does not rejoice in wrongdoing, bears all things, and so on. Jesus' death, on this definition of love, is a far greater expression of love than any other human act. Jesus put it this way: "Greater love has no one than this: to lay down one's life for one's friends." But we need to consider the Cross more closely if we are really to get to the bottom of the answer to the dying soldier's question.

The Sorrow of God

What is God like? Look at the Cross. See Jesus saying to those who taunted and abused and crucified him, "Father, forgive them, for they know not what they do." God is one who is prepared to forgive us even if we crucify his Son, and indeed Jesus died for his tormentors as much as for anyone. What is God like? Look at what Jesus is reported to have said to Saul on the road to Damascus — "Saul, Saul why do you persecute me?" Now we are really getting into deep waters. How could Jesus, enthroned in heaven in a place that we might think is immune to suffering and death, claim to be personally persecuted by Saul? Jesus, of course, had an answer to this during his ministry: "Inasmuch as you have done it unto the least of these you have done it unto me."

We are not told in these stories why we suffer; we are told why Jesus chose to suffer and we are told that there is some deep connection between Jesus' suffering and our suffering, such that even in heaven Jesus suffers with us when his children suffer on earth. This fact led a British chaplain stationed in France during World War I, G. Studdert Kennedy, to some profound reflections on suffering in the form of a poem. The poem, written in the Cockney dialect, is called, "The Sorrow of God." The story in the poem is told from the perspective of an irate older soldier who is angry with God about the waste of a human life, having found a teenage soldier he is fond of dead in the trenches. At first he thinks that God could not possibly be a good or loving God if God would allow such a thing to happen. But then he probes more deeply and says:

> I wonder if God can be sorrowin' still,
> And 'as been all these years.
> I wonder if that's what it really means,
> Not only that 'E once died,
> Not only that 'E came once to earth
> And wept and were crucified?
> Not just that 'E suffered once for all
> To save us from our sins,
> And then went up to 'Is throne on 'igh
> To wait till 'Is heaven begins.
> But what if 'E came to the earth to show,
> By the paths o' pain 'E trod,

The blistering flame of eternal shame
That burns in the heart o' God? . . .
So it isn't just only the crown o' thorns
What 'as pierced and torn God's 'ead;
'E knows the feel uv a bullet, too.
And 'E's 'ad 'Is touch of the lead. . . .
There's a sight o' things what I thought was strange,
As I'm just beginnin' to see:
'Inasmuch as ye did it to one of these
Ye 'ave done it unto Me.' . . .
For the voice of the Lord, as I 'ears it now,
Is the voice of my pals what bled,
And the call of my country's God to me
Is the call of my country's dead.

In this church there are in fact two war memorials — those plaques on the far wall, and the cross hanging over the altar. On this day above all others we recognize the greatest sacrifice ever made, by the Prince of Peace, who still suffers with us even in our suffering for him.

Amen

Them Dry Bones Gonna Rise

Ezekiel 37:1-14

Easter Sunrise Homily

I was somewhere near Durham, England, on Easter Sunday morning, coming to a little Methodist chapel to preach, and the chapel steward raced out of the building to meet me. Breathless, he said, "I am ever so sorry, but I must ask you something." I said, "Go right ahead." "You do believe in the Resurrection, don't you, then? 'Cause the chap who came last year didn't, preached instead on some nonsense about the flowers and annual rebirth in spring." I reassured the man I did indeed believe in resurrection, and I was going to speak not only about Jesus' bodily resurrection long ago on Easter but ours as well. I told him I believed Christ's history was our destiny. He seemed satisfied with that, and the service went on as planned. There's a lot riding on Easter, to say the least, for if Jesus didn't rise we shouldn't be here this early in the morning in a graveyard; indeed I will say, if Jesus didn't rise we *wouldn't* be here this early in the morning. There would be no church, much less a church graveyard.

As we stand here in the cemetery and look across the field at the tombstones, it is not hard to imagine how Ezekiel felt after all those long and hard years in exile when he received the vision of the valley of dry bones. Here before us, like the bones before him, were objects that seemed so lifeless that nothing could animate them. Oh, yes, they could be moved — but not animated, not vivified, not brought to life.

But notice it is not Ezekiel asking the pertinent question, but God — "Son of man, can these bones live?" It would be much the same if I asked you, "Can these tombstones come to life?" Bones, like tombstones, after all, are all about death, not life. When my family once visited Silverton, Colorado, we went to an old Wild West graveyard. One tombstone read, "Here lies the body of Lester Moore/Shot in the back with a .44/No Les, no Moore." Yes, tombstones are all about death. But perhaps you've seen that pizza commercial where they ask, "What do you want on your tombstone?" Tombstone Pizza may be the only kind of tombstone that is all about eating and so about life.

Judging from outward appearances, a somewhat glum Ezekiel decided to defer God's question back to him — and so he responded, "Only you know, O Lord." God indeed does know, for what is impossible for human beings is yet possible, indeed no trouble, for God. Miracles are only surprising to us. For God it's all in a day's work.

Think about it for a moment. Look around you. The sun is coming up, the birds are singing, the flowers are beginning to bloom. No, I will not be preaching on these things, but I think we can look at these things and ask — is it so hard to believe that a God who could create all this big beautiful world could also raise the dead? Is it so hard to conceive that the one who made everything from the smallest flower to the largest galaxy could raise the dead? Surely it requires no more power on God's part, indeed far less — and no more act of imagination on our part if we already believe "the Lord God made it all." Or consider human birth. Is it so hard to believe, having seen the miracle of human birth over and over again, that God could also make possible even physical rebirth? If God gave us life once at birth, could he not repeat the performance later?

To be sure, seeing people rise from the grave is not an everyday experience — but then, miracles never are. They are by definition extraordinary acts of God. The story is told about a county in Ireland in the late Middle Ages that had a problem and had to move a whole cemetery. To the dismay of the vicar, it was discovered during this process that some people had actually been buried alive. Fingernail scratchings on the inside of the wooden coffins were discovered. The vicar noticed that in these cases it was the persons who in life had been the heaviest drinkers. In those days, strong liquor was served in lead tumblers, and heavy drinkers were in danger of going comatose from lead poisoning. Not wanting to see anyone else inadvertently buried alive, the practice of having wakes was instituted — in which comatose Uncle Ned was laid out on the dining room table overnight in hopes that he would wake, hence the name of the event. Ironically, wakes came to be events in which everyone drank too heavily, trying to drown the sorrows of having lost a loved one who did not, in the end, wake up.

But this vicar was ingenious. He decided that a further safeguard was required, and so when a heavy tippler was finally buried, a string was tied to his finger, he was buried in a shallow grave, and the other end of the string was tied to a bell in the graveyard. If he awoke and his finger twitched, he was called a "dead ringer." A watch was posted in the night in case the bell rang then. The person who had the duty was said to be working the "graveyard shift." If the person awoke, and rang the bell, he was said to have been "saved by the bell." This is, of course, a tale of successful resuscitation rather than resurrection, but it is no less surprising than a true miracle. What we are surprised about is no good gauge of what is actually possible, especially for God.

Easter is a time of beauty, but the beauty should no more beguile and distract us than these tombstones should from focusing on the Creator rather than some part of the inanimate creation — whether it be bones or tombstones. God has done more than create this world, and does more than receive us into his arms at death. God has also recreated and redeemed this world through the resurrection of his Son. Through Christ's victory over and beyond death, coming back in a real resurrection body that was tangible and physical though also seems to have had some supernal qualities as well, we learn that God's Yes to life is much louder than death's No. When Christ overcame death it signaled a new order of things, a new phase in God's dealing with us all. God is the one who makes all things new, even old ones.

So, "Can these dry bones live?" We who stand here on Easter morning can do better than that old prophet in exile long before the birth of Jesus. We can say with exuberance and joy, "Yes, they can!" Easter is a fact of history that no one can erase or replace. So what do you want on your tombstone? How about this: "In sure and certain hope of the resurrection!"

Amen

Love's Labor's Won

John 15:9-17; 1 John 5:1-5

Preached at the National Cathedral
in Washington, D.C., May 21, 2006

Feelings, Nothing More Than Feelings

Ours is an affective age. So much is this the case that even the best of counselors often begin their therapy sessions with the question, "How do you feel about this?" or "How does that make you feel?" Feelings are assumed to be the touchstone, the talisman, as it were, of what is really going on in a human life, what really matters. This is so in spite of the fact that we all know that feelings can be tremendously deceptive.

In the earliest days of aviation in America, planes regularly crashed. One of the puzzles was why pilots, when they went into a cloud, would often come out of it in a spin and then crash. One pilot who survived such a crash was interviewed by a reporter and he explained that when he went into the cloud his inner ear, indeed all his sensations, gave him the impression that the plane was not upright or level, and that he needed to bank to the right to be parallel to the ground once more. In fact, this inner sense of his, this strong impression deep inside him, was all wrong, and it was precisely responding to it that led him to bank in such a way that he went into a spin and crashed. Thereafter, altimeters and other gauges were installed in the planes so that pilots could fly even through clouds on a level plane without getting the urge to bank in some precipitous way that would lead to a crash. In the same way, human feelings, even strong ones, are often no good guides to what is true or what is good or even what is helpful.

Ah, but what about the feeling we call love? Surely that feeling is more true, a better barometer and guide to life? Sadly, it often is not so. We could all name persons who have spent — or misspent — their lives following their feelings and their deep desire to be loved, and the result has been one train wreck of a relationship after another. In light of this, one has to ask, "Is the Bible really commanding us to live our lives based on our feelings, even our deepest feelings? Even more profoundly, is Jesus really insisting we do so in one of our Scriptures for today?" In fact, as we will now discover, he is not. Love in the biblical sense, while it certainly involves feelings, is nevertheless not all about feelings; indeed, it is not *primarily* about feelings, as we shall now see. And then, too, the love that is being talked about here has a christological shape, orientation, direction, and source. Jesus is the source, exemplar, director, and object of this love. It is not just any kind of love that is referred to here.

The Command to Love

Have you noticed that in the Bible we are frequently commanded to love? It should have struck us as odd that love is commanded, if we are used to associating love with mere feelings. Jesus says that love of God and of others is the greatest commandment. He even commands us to love our enemies. But is he really ordering our feelings to march in lockstep in a particular direction? Have you ever said to your children, "I demand that for the next three minutes you feel happy and cheerful!" That's rather like that wonderful starfish in *Finding Nemo* commanding itself, "Go to a happy place, go to a happy place, go to a happy place," while the aquarium is being thumped by a mean little girl. If you have tried such an experiment of commanding others' feelings, or even your own, doubtless you have discovered it is an exercise in futility, not fertility. Feelings cannot be commanded. They come and they go and they are subject to the vicissitudes of life, affected and prompted by a thousand different factors — whether we are healthy, whether we are hungry, whether we are sleepy, and a host of other factors.

So here is where I tell you that in the Bible love is normally an action word. It refers to a decision of the will that then leads to an action. Most often it refers to an activity, not a feeling at all. This is why, for example, in the Christian marriage ritual the bride and groom are asked, when it comes to professing their love, to say, "I do," and "I do," and, "I will," and "I will." They are not asked to say, "I feel like it," and, "I feel like it." This should have given us a clue that love is not mainly about feelings, from a biblical point of view. In fact, in Jesus' own words for this morning he tells us, "Greater love has no one than this: to lay down one's life for one's friends." That's love in action, love as a self-sacrificial deed. There are, of course, lesser loves, but Jesus is not speaking of those in this text.

Too often we get real love mixed up with lust, or even just plain desire or loneliness. Young people often say, "We're in love" — but, alas, all too often they are simply "in heat." In fact, the English lexicon is tremendously impoverished when it comes to love. Greek has no less than four or five different words for love — one for physical love (*eros*), one for family love (*storge*), one for brotherly or sisterly love (*philadelphia*), and one for divine love (*agape*). And the love that is being commanded in the New Testament is almost always *agape*. But now you may be saying, "How in the world can Jesus command us to love as God loves? It's hard enough to love like the best of humans; how can we be commanded to love as God does? Isn't that a bridge too far? Should we all be singing now the theme from *Man of La Mancha* — 'To dream the impossible dream. . . .'" Is this command the stuff of fairy tales?

Real Love, a Gift from God

In fact, the answer is No. St. Augustine gives us the clue when he says to God, "Give what you command, Lord, and command whatsoever you will." The capacity to make the decision of the will, to put love into motion, and even to make the ultimate sacrifice, the sacrifice of one's life for others is in fact a gift from God. St. Paul puts it this way when he says that if anyone is in Christ "God has poured out his love into our hearts by the Holy Spirit, whom he has given us" (Rom. 5:5). So let us talk about God's love for a moment.

Victor Furnish, one of the great New Testament scholars of our era, has put the matter in this fashion: "God's love is not like a heat-seeking missile which is triggered by something inherently attractive in the target, the object of love." Indeed not: God loves us when we are unlovely, indeed in some respects seemingly unloveable. God loves us regardless of whether we love God back. God's love is unconditional, in the sense that it is given freely, and not because of anything we have said or done or felt. Indeed, God's love is often given in spite of what we have said or done or felt. It is pure grace — God's unmerited favor, God's undeserved, unearned benefit freely and lavishly poured out by God into our lives. The key, then, is that for human beings to love as God and Jesus have commanded us, they must first be open to receiving that love from God. Paul says it is a matter of believing in Jesus Christ as Lord and receiving the gift of love by means of God's Spirit who comes to indwell the believer.

"Aha!" you may say. "I knew it — so there is a catch. I must first believe, before I can receive, I must first trust before I can have such love." It's not really a catch, though. God is not requiring of you some herculean effort or any sort of *quid pro quo*. It's just that you must unclench your fists and open your hands if you are to catch what he keeps throwing in your direction. No love has ever been received, even of the purely mortal sort, without there first being some trust, some openness, some vulnerability involved. You cannot be loved unless you allow yourself to be loved, and that involves a modicum of trust. But oh, what a wondrous thing it is when you allow yourself to be transformed by God's love! Then, indeed, you are capable of even truly and totally self-sacrificial love. You want proof? I have time for just three brief examples — my wife Ann, Jim Elliot, and Albrecht Dürer.

My wife, unfortunately, is afflicted with periodic migraine headaches, some of which lead to loss of vision for a while in one eye. When my wife has one of those headaches, they are not accompanied by warm, mushy feelings. But when she gets up and prepares a nice meal even in the midst of having such a headache, that, my friends, is love, even though she is feeling horrible. That is love in action, and in this case it is truly and freely given in spite of how she feels. It involves willing and doing, not, in this case, warm, mushy feelings.

Jim Elliot was a missionary to the Waodani Indians in South America, as now portrayed in the movie *The End of the Spear*. It was a dangerous undertaking. In fact, on one furlough he was interviewed by a reporter who asked why he was dealing with such a violent tribe, especially since they seemed so hostile to him and his message. He replied, "He is no fool who gives up what he cannot keep to gain what he cannot lose." He was talking about giving up his own life for these Indians, showing them the love of God in Christ, knowing that even if they took his mortal life, he could not lose the everlasting life God had given him as the ultimate gift of divine love. Shortly after offering this word of wisdom to the reporter, Jim Elliot was martyred by the Waodani Indians. Several decades later, and in fact only a couple of years ago, at a Franklin Graham Crusade in Florida one of my good friends was present when one of the chiefs of the Waodani tribe gave his testimony. He said, "Formerly, I lived badly. But now I live for Jesus, for Jesus sent Jim, and he laid down his life for me. 'Greater love has no one than this: to lay down one's life. . . .'"

Finally I must tell you a truly ultimate love story, a story about Albrecht Dürer, the artist, and his brother.

Back in the fifteenth century, in a tiny village near Nuremberg, lived a family with eighteen children. Eighteen! In order merely to keep food on the table for this mob, the father and head of the household, a goldsmith by profession, worked almost eighteen hours a day at his trade and any other paying chore he could find in the neighborhood. Despite their seemingly hopeless condition, two of the elder children, Albrecht and Albert, had a dream. They both wanted to pursue their talent for art, but they knew full well that their father would never be financially able to send either of them to Nuremberg to study at the academy. After many long discussions at night in their crowded bed, the two boys finally worked out a pact. They would toss a coin. The loser would go down into the nearby mines and, with his earnings, support his brother while he attended the academy. Then, when that brother who won the toss completed his studies, in four years, he would support the other brother at the academy, either with sales of his artwork or, if necessary, also by laboring in the mines. They tossed a coin on a Sunday morning after church. Albrecht Dürer won the toss and went off to Nuremberg.

Albert went down into the dangerous mines and, for the next four years, financed his brother, whose work at the academy was almost an immediate sensation. Albrecht's etchings, his woodcuts, and his oils were far better than those of most of his professors, and by the time he graduated, he was beginning to earn considerable fees for his commissioned works. When the young artist returned to his village, the Dürer family held a festive dinner on their lawn to celebrate Albrecht's triumphant homecoming. After a long and memorable meal, punctuated with music and laughter, Albrecht rose from his honored position at the head of the table to drink a toast to his beloved brother for the years of sacrifice that had enabled Albrecht to fulfill his ambition. His closing words were, "And now, Albert, blessed brother of mine, now it is your turn. Now you can go to Nuremberg to pursue your dream, and I will take care of you." All heads turned in eager expectation to the far end of the table where Albert sat, tears streaming down his pale face, shaking his lowered head from side to side while he sobbed and repeated over and over, "No . . . no . . . no . . . no." Finally, Albert rose and wiped the tears from his cheeks. He glanced down the long table at the faces he loved, and then, holding his hands close to his right cheek, he said softly, "No, brother. I cannot go to Nuremberg. It is too late for me. Look . . . look what four years in the mines have done to my hands! The bones in every finger have been smashed at least once, and lately I have been suffering from arthritis so badly in my right hand that I cannot even hold a glass to return your toast, much less make delicate lines on parchment or canvas with a pen or a brush. No, brother . . . for me it is too late."

More than 450 years have passed. By now, Albrecht Dürer's hundreds of masterful portraits, pen and silver-point sketches, watercolors, charcoals, woodcuts, and copper engravings hang in every great museum in the world, but the odds are great that you, like most people, are familiar with only one of Albrecht Dürer's works. More than merely being familiar with it, you very well may have a reproduction hanging in your home or office. One day, to pay homage to Albert for all that he had sacrificed, Albrecht Dürer painstakingly drew his brother's abused hands with palms together and thin fingers stretched skyward. He called his powerful drawing simply *Hands,* but the entire world almost immediately opened their hearts to his great masterpiece and renamed his tribute of love *The Praying Hands.* These were the hands of genuine, painful, suffering love, the same sort of hands we see on the Christ with arms outstretched to the world while on the Cross and saying, "Father, forgive them, they know not what they do."

You see, in the end biblical love is all about action, not talk. When it talks about love, it is all about self-sacrifice not self-aggrandizement or self-fulfillment, though if you love in this sacrificial way one by-product is that you indeed will be fulfilled, in fact you will be filled up to the full with God's love, as God has an endless supply. In the end it's all about love's labor's won, not lost. It is this sort of love that makes the world go round, and indeed makes life worth living. It is this sort of love that is both given and then commanded by God. And best of all, God long ago sent his one and only Son so that we might have love and have it in abundance. Jesus lived and died not merely to make real love possible, but to make it abundantly available to whosoever will believe on him unto everlasting life.

Amen

For Study and Meditation

"Fool's Goal"
(Psalm 14 and Luke 16:19-31)

- Confess to the Lord your need for him and your desire to live wholly, only for him. Confess to him those times you have foolishly chosen the things of the world over him. Ask him to deliver you from dependence on anyone or anything but him.
- Journal about your journey of faith. Map out your spiritual journey — ups and downs — recalling specific moments in which you experienced the real presence of Christ in your life. Allow yourself to work on this for several days. Record everything that comes to mind in detail so that you can return to this again and again.
- Pray for persons you know who are atheists and for those who have yet to hear the truth. Ask God to show you how you might be an instrument of his grace and mercy in these people's lives.

THOUGHTS FOR FURTHER REFLECTION

"Creatures created in God's image will always hear the whispering inside, even in their innermost being, that God exists."

Ben Witherington III

"All human beings living in a fallen world are terminal, and it is only a fool, not a wise person, who does not live keeping this fact steadily in view."

Ben Witherington III

"Blessed are those who know their need for God."

Ben Witherington III

"Sincere — Sin's Here"
(2 Samuel 11:2-27 and 12:1-7; Psalm 51)

♦ Meditate on Psalm 51 after reading through it several times. Place yourself in this familiar psalm, replacing the personal pronouns with your own name.

♦ Memorize Psalm 51:10-12 and/or Psalm 51:15-17. It might help to rewrite these verses (keeping the original meaning) in your own words. Post them somewhere in your home or office as you commit these words to memory.

♦ Worship the Lord, thanking him for grace and forgiveness this day. Sing favorite songs of praise to him, or simply listen to a favorite CD of songs that recount God's grace and forgiveness. Feel free to invite others to share in this time of worship and reflection on the great grace of our God.

THOUGHTS FOR FURTHER REFLECTION

"Confession itself is not the cure nor the cleansing — God provides that."

Ben Witherington III

"To be sure, what God is looking for is not merely nice persons, but new creatures transformed by his grace."

Ben Witherington III

"The man who has God for his treasure has all things in One."

A. W. Tozer

"O Jesus, my feet are dirty. Come even as a slave to me, pour water into your bowl, come and wash my feet. . . ."

Origen of Alexandria (185-254)

"The Temptations of God"
(Matthew 4:1-11; Luke 4:1-13)

♦ Fast and pray about areas of temptation in your life. Take 24 hours to fast from food or something else that consumes a significant amount of your time or thoughts (for example, music, television, Internet). Remember to enter your fast "full of the Spirit" as Jesus did during his time in the wilderness. It might help to carry your journal around to reflect on what God reveals to you and how you feel during this time.

♦ Memorize a passage of Scripture that might strengthen you in your own time of temptation. You might consider Psalm 16:1, Psalm 86:2, Habakkuk 3:19, 1 Corinthians 10:12-14, or 2 Thessalonians 3:3. As you memorize the words of the passage you choose, allow the words to find a place in your heart. Remember that Scripture memory, submission to the Word, and reliance on the Spirit *together* help you to successfully navigate temptations.

♦ Pray through Psalm 121. Read it slowly and deliberately, taking in each promise. It might help to personalize the psalm by writing it in your own words. Allow these words to take root in your heart and sustain you through the days ahead.

THOUGHTS FOR FURTHER REFLECTION

"Life is the proving ground of discipleship and I guarantee you that the temptations we face now will come back to haunt us later if we do not resist them repeatedly and vigorously."

Ben Witherington III

"The greatest of human temptations is always to worship something as God that is less than and other than God."

Ben Witherington III

"The more troubles I meet, the more convinced I am that I do the will of God."

Francis Asbury

"I am not here to realize myself, but to know Jesus."

Oswald Chambers

"The Sorrow of God"
(Isaiah 53:1-12)

- ◆ Study and meditate on Isaiah 53:1-12 and the sacrifice made on the cross. Record your thoughts in your journal or in the form of an original poem, painting, or other creative work.
- ◆ Solitude is a beautiful, often misunderstood spiritual discipline. The spiritual discipline of solitude can be described as a sort of fast from the clamor and noise of the world. Spend at least fifteen minutes in silence and solitude today. Allow yourself to simply *be* in the presence of the Lord. Let him lavish his extraordinary love on you as you sit still before him and reflect upon the Cross.

THOUGHTS FOR FURTHER REFLECTION

"If you think it is easy for God to forgive sin, take a good hard look at the Cross."

Ben Witherington III

"The cross of Christ is the most revolutionary thing ever to appear among men."

A. W. Tozer

"To know the cross is not merely to know our own sufferings. For the cross is the sign of salvation, and no one is saved by his own sufferings. To know the cross is to know that we are saved by the sufferings of Christ. It is, then, to know Christ."

Thomas Merton

"Thanks be to thee, O Lord Jesus Christ, for all the benefits which thou hast given us; for all the pains and insults which thou has borne for us. O most merciful redeemer, friend, and brother, may we know thee more clearly, love thee more dearly, and follow they more nearly; for thine own sake."

Richard of Chichester

"Them Dry Bones Gonna Rise"
(Ezekiel 37:1-14)

♦ Study and meditate on Ezekiel 37:1-14. Read through the passage at least two times. Meditate on Ezekiel's experience in the valley of dry bones. The description of the dry bones coming to life in this passage is riveting and powerful. How has God done similar work in your life and the lives of the people around you?

♦ Journal through your time of study and meditation. Candidly express the thoughts that enter your head as you read through this passage. What images come to mind in your own life and experiences? Write or draw to express your thoughts.

♦ Worship the Lord, thanking him for receiving and redeeming you. Praise God for his resurrection power in your life. Praise him for the victory. Praise him for his faithfulness. Through Scripture, prayer, and song, worship our God!

THOUGHTS FOR FURTHER REFLECTION

"Miracles are only surprising to us. For God, it's all in a day's work."

Ben Witherington III

"God's Yes to life is much louder than death's No."

Ben Witherington III

"You awaken us to delight in Your presence and praises; for you made us for Yourself and our heart is restless until it rests in You."

St. Augustine

"Lord, you know what is best; let this be done or that be done as you please. Give what you will, as much as you will, when you will. Do with me as you know best, as will most please you, and will be for your greater honor. Place me where you will and deal with me freely in all things. I am in your hand; turn me about whichever way you will. Behold, I am your servant, ready to obey in all things. Not for myself do I desire to live, but for you — would that I could do this worthily and perfectly!"

Thomas à Kempis

"Love's Labors Won"
(John 15:9-17 and 1 John 5:1-5)

◆ Spend some time volunteering, perhaps at a shelter or soup kitchen or nursing home in your area. As you do, be mindful of Jesus' teaching that love is an action rather than a feeling.
◆ Journal about a time when someone showed you the love of Christ through his or her actions.
◆ Spend some time in prayer, thanking God for sending Jesus as a perfect example of love in action. Then thank God for other people in your life who have embodied this kind of love.

THOUGHTS FOR FURTHER REFLECTION

"God has poured out his love into our hearts by the Holy Spirit, whom he has given us."

Romans 5:5

"You cannot be loved unless you allow yourself to be loved, and that involves a modicum of trust. But oh, what a wondrous thing it is when you allow yourself to be transformed by God's love! Then, indeed, you are capable of even truly and totally self-sacrificial love."

Ben Witherington III

"Give what you command, Lord, and command whatsoever you will."

St. Augustine

PENTECOST

The Light Bursts into Flame

The God-Whispered Words

1 Kings 19:1-18

A Bad Day at the Office for a Court Prophet

There is a wonderful little person named Ziggy who has appeared in the comic strips in the daily papers for many years. He's "vertically challenged" and many seem to identify with him because he's often the underdog, or a "lovable loser" like Charlie Brown. There is one Ziggy strip in particular that sort of epitomizes the way he views the world. He and his small dog are looking out the window of their high-rise apartment in a major downtown area of a metropolis. They see the hustle and bustle of the busy streets below and the sun rising over the skyscrapers on another day, and Ziggy turns to his dog and says, "Well, it looks like it's you and me against the world, and I think we are going to get creamed!"

This is precisely the position we find Elijah in at the beginning of our story for this morning. Elijah, though he was no loser — indeed he had just had a major victory over the prophets of Baal — was in a tense situation. He had been summoned by Queen Jezebel, an ardent supporter of those prophets of Baal, and she had threatened his life. Elijah knew it was a serious threat, and he became very much unnerved and fled. His fleeing could not be called a strategy to get perspective; it was an escape plan, pure and simple. Nevertheless, he needed to get away from the problem, and get to a place where he could hear God's answer to the problem. This is often a good policy for us. Sometimes it is better to step back from a problem to get a better perspective. The Lebanese poet Khalil Gibran puts it this way: "The mountain, to the climber, is clearer from the plain."

Premises Vacated, No Forwarding Address

The text says that Elijah fled to Beersheba — which is to say he fled all the way from northern Israel, through Judea, to the southernmost city in Judea — left his servant there in Beersheba, and went off into the desert to pray. It is very clear that when Elijah wanted to get away, he wanted to get very far away. But what did he pray for? Elijah was so despondent and depressed that he said to God in essence, "There is no profit in being a true prophet. Take my life, Lord, I don't deserve to live longer than my ancestors." What had so depressed Elijah that he wanted to lie down and die? He tells us very directly: "I have been very zealous for the LORD, and yet the Israelites have rejected your covenant, broken down your altars, and put your prophets to death. I alone am left, and now they are even trying to kill me." Elijah is in effect telling God, "It's you and me against the world and I think we are going to get creamed!"

How often have any one of us been in this sort of position, or at least felt we were? At the end of our ropes, ready to give up, maybe ready to lie down and die. The prophet Elijah sits under a broom tree in the desert and laments that there are no converts, so he might as well die. Contrast him with the prophet Jonah, who sits under his vine and complains to God because all of Nineveh is converted — and so he might as well die! It's a wonder how God puts up with his messengers; they're not pleased when things seem to go wrong, and they are still not pleased if God fulfills his word and things go right.

Despite his depression, however, Elijah did the right thing. He prayed to God in his hour of need. One wonders how many suicides have been averted by desperate individuals putting themselves in God's hands rather than making a noose when they reach the end of their rope. Elijah doesn't attempt to end his life; he places it back in the hands of his Maker. It is interesting that at this juncture Elijah is showing all the classic signs of depression — he does not take good care of himself, he has worn himself out with fear, running, failing to eat. At the point of both physical and emotional exhaustion, he prays to God and instead of dying he falls asleep. Shakespeare once said that sleep "knits up the raveled sleeve of care — sleep, the best medicine." But what happened next?

The Problem with Answered Prayer

One of the more fallacious things one could say about God is that sometimes God does not answer prayers. The assumption behind this statement is that only an affirmative answer counts as an answer to prayer. But, in fact, No is just as much an answer to prayer as Yes is. It is characteristic of the biblical God that he answers our prayers not at the point of our request, but rather at the point of our needs, for God knows far better than we do what is best for us. The story is told of a little girl who lived in an apartment in Cleveland. She had been praying to God for a pony, a real pony, for Christmas. She shared this desire with her grandmother while she was visiting her in the country, not long before Christmas. They were making chocolate chip cookies together, and the grandmother was wise enough to say to her granddaughter, "Well, dear, when you come back to see me again in January, you tell me how things turn out about the pony." Christmas came and went, and the little girl did not, not surprisingly, get the pony. There was nowhere to put it in her family's apartment. When she visited her grandmother again, the grandmother gingerly and gradually brought the conversation around to the sore subject and asked, "Well, did God answer your prayer about the pony?" The little girl looked incredulously at her grandmother and replied promptly, "Oh, yes, Grannie, God said No." No is, after all, an answer to prayer, and No is the answer that God gave Elijah when he asked God to take his life.

The Lord knew that the real answer to Elijah's problems and to his depression was not to take away his life, but rather to strengthen it — to give him sustenance, support, assurance. These sorts of things can get a person back on the right track. God ministered to Elijah not at the point of his request, but at the point of his actual need. So we are told that first of all one of God's angels provided Elijah with food and drink, reviving him physically so he could in fact take a very long pilgrimage so as to deal with the spiritual and emotional parts of his problem.

Mt. Horeb is another name for Mt. Sinai, where God had famously told Moses, "Take two tablets and call me in the morning." God knew that the gift of physical food, however miraculously provided, was not enough to minister to all of Elijah's problems. Likewise, we too must go deeper to heal the hurts of the heart. Notice that God does not stop ministering to Elijah until he is truly revived and ready to go again. Neither will God treat us in any less holistic a way. The *shalom* that comes from God involves the well-being of the whole person.

That Mountaintop Experience

When Elijah got to Horeb, it was time to minister to the spiritual part of the problem. It is best for all of us when we have a problem to go somewhere quiet where we can be alone and talk with God and try to sort things out through prayer, a personal conversation with God. Notice how God asks Elijah why he has come to Horeb, as if trying to stimulate the conversation. Actually, the point is to get Elijah to open up and share what is bothering him so much. God wanted Elijah to realize what he was actually running from so he could see the real source of his difficulties. As it turns out, Elijah's real problem was his own fears — he was afraid of dying a pointless death at the hands of those who should have respected and listened to him as God's prophet. Put another way, he was afraid of being publicly shamed and feeling as if he had accomplished little in his ministry. Having named his fear, and unburdened his soul, Elijah was finally ready to hear God's solution to the problem. All too often we do not hear God's solution to our problems because 1) we are too busy complaining to hear the still, small voice; 2) we do not really admit, due to pride, that we have a problem: we are in denial; or 3) we secretly prefer sympathy rather than solutions that would stop the flow of comfort and consolation from others.

What follows is one of the great passages in the Old Testament, in which we learn something very clear about how God's will and answers can be found, even in troubling situations. We are told that there was a mighty wind, but that God and his will could not be discerned in the wind. There was also a great earthquake, but again God's design and word could not be read in the earthquake. There was a conflagration, but, however dazzling, it revealed nothing of God's real nature or will for the situation. Then, finally, there was a still, small voice, a bare whisper, like a breath of wind, which one had to be totally still and concentrate in order to hear.

At this juncture God calls Elijah by name, and Elijah wraps his mantle around his head, and goes forth from the cave to an open spot. Notice that the first direct revelation involves calling Elijah by his personal name. Some time ago I received one of those form letters in the mail from Time Inc. It was of the usual sort, in which they would leave blank spaces in a form letter and then type the person's name in every so often to make it look personal. Unfortunately the task in this case was apparently left to a computer who deduced that the name "Dr. Ben Witherington III" would never fit in the allotted space. Thus the letter read (I kid you not):

> Dear Dr. Third:
>
> We know you are one of the most important persons in your area, and so we are making this personal appeal to you to renew your subscription to *Time*. Dr. Third, surely you do not wish to miss a single issue, so that you may keep abreast of foreign and domestic affairs as you have in the past. So please, Dr. Third, consider this our personal appeal to renew now by filling in your name on the form below, making sure it reads "Dr. Third" as it has in the past.
>
> *Yours sincerely,*
> Time Inc.

I was tempted to write them back — "Dear Inc. . . ." You see, when the world tries to be personal it treats persons like numbers and things. But when God is personal, he calls us by name, just as God did with Elijah. We have been informed that nature in itself is not the voice of God, and God's will cannot be discerned directly by reading the book of creation. One must place oneself where one can hear God's word — whether on a mountaintop or in a church or synagogue. And both prayer and listening, as well as consulting God's word, are involved.

And So?

After all this, God reassured Elijah by saying, "You are not alone. There are other true believers around, even where you are ministering. Carry on with the tasks I have given you, and I will provide you with some extra help." It is amazing how much help just a reassurance that we are not alone can be, grasping that God has not abandoned us in a difficult situation. Sometimes we may feel we are one of the few truly loyal persons in our church or locale. God can show us it is not so. Thus, we should not give up or become depressed; we should return to the "rock from which we were hewn" and see what God has to say about the situation. When we face difficulties we stick to the task, stay in it, and speak out, rather than get out and have nothing more to say. Like Elijah, we are called to work with God's people, even if they are recalcitrant and even threatening. And when we get down we can turn to prayer, knowing that God will send others to help, for the God who revealed himself to Elijah on Horeb and called him out of his depression can do the same for us now, if we are willing to place ourselves where it is quiet enough to hear — hear the God-whispered words from the still, small voice.

Amen

Chariot of Fire

Ezekiel 1

Down in the Dumps

Imagine, if you will, a man who is down in the dumps, and stuck in a foreign country. He is a man who had shown great promise in his youth, being the son of a priest in Jerusalem and destined for the priesthood himself. For Hebrews there were few honors greater than this. Imagine, however, that this man, along with a host of other notable Jews in Jerusalem, had been taken prisoner by the famous Babylonian King Nebuchadnezzar and his army and carted off into exile in about 598 B.C. to the sweltering marshlands in the middle of the Fertile Crescent, in what is today called Iraq. There they were settled by an irrigation canal called the Kebar.

Ezekiel was a married man and the appointed leader of his people. He had been reared in the Temple precincts in Jerusalem, anticipating the day he would become a priest. But here he is eking out a bare existence by the Kebar. Perhaps he is brooding over his ill fortune, because our text for today says quite clearly that he had just turned thirty, the age priests became vested and began to take on their ministry. Stuck out in the boondocks, a man outside of and to some extent without a country, bereft of his life calling, Ezekiel cannot have been anticipating what would happen on this particular birthday.

But God has ways of using us even when we think we are useless, even in ways we would never have expected, and this is not necessarily because we have hidden talents, but because God can do a new thing in our lives, equipping us with new abilities and a new calling. On his birthday in 593

B.C. Ezekiel, having lived in Babylon for five years, was called to be a prophet instead of a priest, in a manner that will remind you of what happened to Paul on the road to Damascus. Both men saw a remarkable vision that utterly changed the course of their lives. Ezekiel's close encounter with God involved a throne-chariot vision that was so overwhelming that it left him temporarily mute and paralyzed. The story will bear some close scrutiny.

Down from the Sky

Many of you will no doubt have seen the old Steven Spielberg movie *Close Encounters of the First Kind.* Near the close of the movie there is an amazing scene in which a giant spacecraft with multicolored lights and all sorts of metal projectiles on it slowly descends from the sky at a spot where scientists are waiting with their instruments to monitor the encounter and try to communicate with the visitors from outer space. This spaceship is so huge it is virtually the size of a mountain and yet it floats down as gentle as a balloon in a breeze. The human beings who see this are completely awestruck and dumbfounded, standing there with their mouths hanging open.

It was like that for Ezekiel as well. There he was, sitting by his irrigation ditch, minding his own business, when suddenly he looked up and noticed some stormclouds on the horizon. He saw the black clouds and the lightning that began flashing from them towards earth. But then this magnificent natural wonder gave way to a supernatural one. Ezekiel saw God's throne-chariot descending from the sky and with it God in person. This was no mere close encounter with aliens from outer space. The only alien present was Ezekiel, the Hebrew in Babylon. This was an encounter with the Lord God himself, creator of the universe, who always was, is, and always will be.

Ezekiel tries to give us a detailed description of the sight, but if we are to get any sense or idea of what he saw we will need to use our imaginations. He keeps groping for words, using the phrase "it was like," as is so characteristic of the descriptions of apocalyptic visions in the Bible. So imagine four creatures with basically a human form, yet with four faces and four wings each, and with animal-like feet. These living creatures were upholding a platform on which the throne and God's presence were to be found. We are apparently meant to think of the Ark of the Covenant in the Holy of Holies in Jerusalem, with the cherubim holding up what was above them. The creatures each had four faces — the face of a human being, the face of a lion, the face of an ox, and the face of an eagle. Two of the wings of each creature were used to cover their bodies and two were extended at right angles so they touched the outstretched wings of the creature next to them, forming something of a square or cube formation with wheels in between them.

These wheels were also on each of the four sides, like the creatures, and apparently each wheel was intersected by another wheel. The creatures gleamed like polished metal and in the middle of the creatures, underneath the platform, fire or lightning could be seen flashing. In the rims of the wheels one could see eyes, a frightening sight, eyes that were looking in all directions. The platform above the heads of the creatures was vast and looked like a sheet of ice. The throne on top of the platform appeared to be made of some sort of blue precious stones. Seated on the throne was a figure that looked like a human being, yet in some ways did not look human. The best Ezekiel can do is say "it was like" and "it was like," because he had never seen anything like this before. He had never had a vision before, so far as we can tell, and wasn't expecting to become a visionary on his birthday. The person on the throne was engulfed in a dazzling blur of light that appeared like a rainbow of colors. This entire throne-chariot was constantly moving as one unit, with God's Spirit or breath or wind (the Hebrew word used here, *ruach,* can mean any of these things) motivating and moving and directing the whole thing.

This vision was so overwhelming that Ezekiel fell to the ground. Somehow he had experienced a glorious vision of God and lived. That in itself was something of a miracle since Israel had been previously warned that no human being could look on God and live. But what in the world was the significance of this vision? Why had the God of Israel, the God enthroned previously in Jerusalem, shown up in Babylon by an irrigation ditch?

Down to Earth

To understand the significance of this vision you must first bear in mind that Israelites had often been guilty of thinking that God was their personal possession, confined to the land of Israel, indeed confined to the Temple in Jerusalem. Secondly, after five years in exile, it is easy to understand how Jews might think God had abandoned them, or at least that God seemed powerless to help them. Their prior understanding of God was often that he was a great big security blanket who would protect them when their enemies attacked, or perhaps he was like a parachute who would always soften the landing when they were busy bailing out or tumbling into trouble. Neither of these ideas was correct.

When Ezekiel saw this vision it must have dawned on him that: 1) God was alive; and 2) God was as much a God in Babylon as he was in Judea; and 3) that he still cared for his people, for he was now appearing in splendor to one of their number. This vision of a mobile throne indicated clearly that God was not confined to one place or nation, and of course besides omnipresence the many eyes looking in all directions suggest a God who is all-knowing. He had not overlooked the plight of his people. The ability of the throne chariot to move in any direction effortlessly, with its wheels pointing in all four directions, indicates God's power and control over all things and beings. This is also indicated by the creatures with four wings. The rabbis who interpreted this text said that the human was supreme above all other creatures, the lion was king among wild animals, the ox was supreme among domesticated beasts, and the eagle was chief of the birds of the air. Thus this vision suggests that God is Lord over all creation, and that in turn all creatures are and should be lifting up God who reigns on his throne above. All creatures great and small are to exalt and serve this God. Then, too, the vision suggests that it is God's Spirit who motivates and guides these creatures and it is their task to do God's bidding. Thus we see clearly a vision of a God who is all-powerful, all-seeing, and omnipresent. Here indeed is a strange and wonderful vision!

What It All Comes Down To

All of this may seem to us to be far removed from our own personal or religious experiences. It may seem to be a weird experience that happened long ago and far away to someone who is a stranger to us. But the truth of the matter is that the God of Ezekiel is our God as well, and that God has not changed. God is still a mighty and all-knowing and caring God, vitally concerned about our lives. And people today are still having some amazing experiences of God. Nor has our need for God changed — we still need God's presence, power, guidance, love in our lives, perhaps especially when we are resident aliens.

In 1979 my wife and I were living in Durham, England, and we were expecting our first child. We had gone through Lamaze classes, and my wife, who is a biologist, and I wanted to have this baby in the natural way, without the use of drugs. We wanted to avoid the "knock 'em out and drag 'em out" method of delivering our firstborn because of the potential harmful effects it has on the newborn. Some weeks before the scheduled date of our daughter's birth, Ann's blood pressure began to soar and then, suddenly, three weeks before the due date, the doctors insisted she be placed in the hospital. The day came when her blood pressure was so extreme that the doctor told Ann they were going to have to induce labor, and she was distraught. I remember vividly going to the hospital that night, and we were doing our devotions together, reading through the book of Ezekiel, as it happened. We were reading from much later in the book, in the midst of the "doom and gloom" chapters of the book, and yet three phrases stuck out as promises to those in an alien land: "and I will multiply your kindred," "and I will keep you safe," "and you will return home soon." I turned to Ann and said, "Don't worry, honey, the baby is on the way." She looked at me and said, "You really think so?" I said, "There must be some reason we waded through all those judgment oracles tonight to find those nuggets." I went home convinced that our child would be born soon.

When I got back to our house I simply remained dressed and paced the floor. We had neither car nor phone, but our friend Bob Raymond had both, so he was the one the hospital called. Suddenly, at four in the morning, Bob was banging on the door. He was stunned to see me standing there dressed and ready to go to the hospital. He asked, "How did you know to be ready?" I said, "Ezekiel warned us this was about to happen." Now, of course I knew that Ezekiel was speaking quite literally to the exiles about their return from exile and the replenishing of their decimated population, but God had used those ancient promises on the night of August 13, 1979, to make clear what the divine plan was in our lives. Sure enough, Christy was safely born later that morning of August 14, very much alert and full of life and delivered without the aid of drugs. But this is not the end of the story.

Not only had God come to us, as he had to Ezekiel, in a foreign land with a message of hope and regeneration, but God on that very day provided family. Late on the afternoon of August 14 a knock came on the caretaker's cottage door, and there stood our American friends Tom and

Marylee Albin, who were studying in southern England in Cambridge. Was it just an accident that they showed up on this day? Surely not, and Marylee immediately said, "Well, now you have some family and friends here to celebrate on this day, and we will help you with cooking and cleaning." But that was not all. Even later that day another knock came on the door in Durham, and there before me stood a very scruffy-looking young man with a huge pack on his back. He told me he had been hitchhiking all over Europe and had heard that my wife was here in Durham so he thought he would stop by for a visit — on this day of all days. He was a former high school student of my wife's in South Hamilton, Massachusetts. What a 24-hour period it had been for Ann and me and our new family!

John Muir, the American naturalist, once said words to the effect of, "We look at life from the back side of the tapestry. And what we usually see is loose ends, knots, dangling threads. But occasionally light shines through the tapestry, and we get a glimpse of the larger design, of the darks and lights woven together into something beautiful." August 13 and 14, 1979, when our daughter was born, was one of those days in our lives, just as Ezekiel had such a day on his birthday in 593 B.C. You see, this amazing vision of Ezekiel, like my reading of the Word from Ezekiel over 2500 years later, was meant to tell us that God is still with us, still in control. God is still in the process of revealing himself to us, to those who will receive and believe his visions and words. Furthermore, he is still commissioning us.

This God-moment in Ezekiel's life was life-changing; indeed, one could say life-shattering. It even had temporary physical side effects. Though Ezekiel recovered physically, spiritually, and otherwise, he was never the same person again, any more than Ann and I have been the same since Christy came into the world. Ezekiel was now called to be a prophet, to proclaim God's word whether it was well- or ill-received. Ezekiel was an ordinary person who had an extraordinary experience of God's presence, a presence that was powerful and life-changing in a positive way.

Ezekiel realized from this that he could no longer dwell in or on the past, no longer focus on past glories, for he had seen Glory in person in the present. He had to proclaim that there was a future beyond the exile, and it even involved dry bones being raised up and being given new life. There was no time for looking back in longing, or with regret or in reverie. Ezekiel saw the wheels and the vision led him into a lifetime of service to God. Likewise, that day in 1979 galvanized me, reminded me that God was with me, and I went on to finish my doctoral work and become a teacher of the New Testament. When suddenly God reveals his glory and sovereignty over the vicissitudes of life, even if it is a momentary glimpse of the larger design of things, one is never the same thereafter.

As it was with Ezekiel, so it is with us today. God will break into our consciousness, will rearrange our priorities, will change our mood, will equip us for ministry, will refurbish our memories, and will guide, guard, and impel us into the future in such a fashion that we can say with Ezekiel, and that famous missionary Adoniram Judson: "Though things seem dark now, the future is as bright as the promises of God."

Amen

Transfixed

Revelation 21:1–22:5

The Longing for Home

Have you ever really longed to go home? You've been away for a long time, and you miss the friends, the family, the food, the physical landscape that spells home. You miss that profound sense of being at home, at rest, in sanctuary, secure, and beyond reproach. Far from the madding crowd, far from the busyness and anxieties of life.

In his beautiful poem "Heaven–Haven" Gerard Manley Hopkins puts it this way:

> I have desired to go
> Where springs not fail,
> To fields where flies no sharp and sided hail
> And a few lilies blow.
>
> And I have asked to be
> Where no storms come,
> Where the green swell is in the havens dumb,
> And out of the swing of the sea.

Frederick Buechner in his powerful book *The Longing for Home* speaks of the primal nature of the longing for home. He reminds us of our clichés: "There's no place like home," the words spoken by Dorothy when she was in Oz and so very much longed to go back to Kansas. But of that home from which we have come, Thomas Wolfe, that great North Carolina novelist, says "You can't go home again." You may miss it, long for it, seek it, but it cannot be your destination as a Christian person. But oh how powerfully does it tug at our hearts, this home from whence we have come. In the fall of 2003 I was assisting with a retreat for Asbury Seminary at the Cove, Billy Graham's retreat center, but on Saturday afternoon the sun came out and I took a busload of our friends on a ride on the Blue Ridge Parkway. The sun was shining, the sky was brilliant Carolina blue, the leaves were turning yellow and orange, and the vistas were grand. In my heart I said, "I am home" for I had been living outside my home state for twenty years. And yet I knew that however beautiful the North Carolina mountains were, they were not my permanent home — indeed, I could never fully go back to my birth home.

The Christian journey, you see, is not finally a journey back, but a journey forward. It has been said that a Jew is a person who faces the past and backs his way into the future saying, "Tradition, tradition, tradition," while a Christian is a person who looks forward and reminds herself that "the future is as bright as the promises of God." While this contrast between the Jew and the Christian is certainly only partially true, it is striking to me that Jews of John's day didn't necessarily see life that way. Consider the following quote from *4 Ezra*, a Jewish work written almost at the same time as John's Apocalypse: "For many miseries will affect those who inhabit the world in the last times, because they have walked in great pride. But it is for you that Paradise is opened, the tree of life is planted, the age to come is prepared, plenty is provided, a city is built, rest is appointed, goodness is established, and wisdom is perfected beforehand" (8:48-52).

John's Dream Home

Today it is our task to examine John of Patmos's "dream home," the destiny and destination to which he has been pointed in his vision and to which he points us. John knows that God has put in the heart of every human a homesickness that can only be cured by entering the new Jerusalem. Stuck on a godforsaken island, in exile from home and hearth and friends and family, John dreams a big dream of an eternal home, a dream home that was once in heaven, but shall become heaven on earth when Christ returns. It is not a surprise that when John describes this place, this home, this final destination, that he thinks of both a beautiful garden like Eden unspoiled, and a grand city like Jerusalem untainted by sin and sorrow and suffering, free from disease, decay, and death. He does not see our destination as an escape into a safe haven far away from humanity like a wildlife sanctuary or a monastery, but rather a pilgrimage into the midst of a city full of people, a city that also contains a garden.

It is as if the monastery and the wildlife sanctuary have been incorporated into the city successfully. In other words, it is as if finally the harmony between nature and human nature, the peace between human beings and God, has finally been achieved in the presence of the radiant Christ, the bridegroom. But that is not all, for not only does the bridegroom come walking down the stairsteps of heaven to meet the bride, but the heavenly city, the saints and all that is in it comes with him. Heaven comes down, and glory will fill our souls. Our ultimate destiny is not, nor has it ever been, to live in a disembodied condition in heaven, forever-and-ever-amen. Our ultimate destiny is to be fully conformed to the image of Christ by means of resurrection, and thereby made fit to dwell in the new Jerusalem, the holy city, in which there will be no more sin or suffering or sorrow or disease or decay or death or war or weapons or violence.

Think of it! A hometown with no need of hospital, no need of police, no need of walls save for ceremonial purposes, no need of firemen or insurance agents, no house of worship in its midst, for the division between the sacred and the secular will be obliterated forever: all the land will be our Father's land, and all the city will be holy and light, and in it there will be no shadow of turning, no darkness at all, for in him there is no darkness at all. It will be the ultimate family reunion, the ultimate marriage celebration, the ultimate triumph of all that is good and true and beautiful and loving over all that is wicked and false and ugly and hateful. We will not study war any more, we will not need a Department of Homeland Security, we will not need politicians to tell us what is best, we will not need to be pointed toward God, for we will be dwelling right in his midst. Faith will become sight, hope will be realized, and perfect love will cast out all fear. Don't you want to go home? Don't you want to be there? John is saying to us, "Don't sell your ticket to the final destination for the lesser good of dying and going to be with Jesus."

Eugene Peterson puts it this way: "Many people want to go to heaven the way they want to go to Florida: they think the weather will be an improvement and the people decent. But the biblical final destination is not merely heaven, it is new heaven and new earth. It is not a nice environment far removed from the stress of the hard city life. It is the invasion of the earthly city by the heavenly one. We enter this final destination not by escaping what we do not like but by the sanctification of the place in which God has placed us." We enter this final destination by finally being fully conformed to the image of Christ by means of a resurrection. Then, then indeed we may talk in the full sense of Christian perfection, nothing less than the full conformity to the image of Christ in body as well as in mind and spirit and emotions. Don't you want to be there? Don't you want to go home?

This home is not achieved, it is received. It is not accomplished, it is entered by grace through faith. It is a city in which God himself condescends and there is a corporate merger between heaven and earth, and God in person will personally wipe away every tear from every eye. The future is so bright that we will all need shades, as we are told there will be no more night. The future is so bright that in this city we will not only have all we need, we will have all we want and want only all we have. And we will reign forever and ever on earth with our God and with his Christ.

Homecoming — or Rest Stop Along the Way?

Some years ago I was called upon to do the funeral service for my grandfather in Wilmington, North Carolina. He had lived a long rich life, into his nineties, and had been a devout Christian and lifelong member of his local Baptist church. I remember when I was small asking him with some fear and trepidation why he had been such a "straight arrow" in life, so to speak. He told me, "Heaven is too sweet, and hell is too hot, to mess around in this life." That stuck with me through these many years. He had his eye on the afterlife, and he lived his earthly life with at least one eye always on that horizon, just as John is encouraging us to do in our text for today. The time came for the interment service at the old graveyard, and the funeral directors were about to crank my grandfather down into the ground, when an impulse struck me. I had not seen Pop, as I had arrived after the visiting hours and the casket had been closed throughout the service in the church and at the graveyard. I asked them to open the casket for a moment, and I went over and kissed my grandfather on the forehead and said, "Goodbye, Pop." But then I thought — No. He is not gone, he has just gone on to the heavenly resting station. I decided that instead of goodbye I would say what I had learned from John: "I'll see you at home."

Our final destiny and privilege and task is indeed to adore and love God and enjoy him forever, casting down our golden crowns before the glassy sea. With the whole company of heaven, with all the saints of the past and now we experience: Exultation, adoration, celebration, jubilation, coronation, destination all wrapped into one. Don't you want to be there? Don't you want to go home? I cannot speak for you, but as for me — I want to go home, and I want home to be just as John described it.

Amen

For Study and Meditation

"The God-Whispered Words"
(1 Kings 19:1-18)

+ Silence is an integral part of intimate prayer. Take 15 minutes (more as you are able) and go somewhere you can be completely alone and quiet.
+ Pray candidly and freely to God as Elijah did in our passage. Allow yourself to speak openly and honestly with God, holding nothing back. If words do not come easily, simply sit still and spend more time in silence before the Lord. Take time to *listen* to what God might be trying to say to you during your time of prayer.
+ Journal your thoughts regarding the passage from 1 Kings 19:1-18 and the sermon. Reflect on a time in your life when you have felt a little like Elijah, at the end of your rope. Reflect on God's faithful answers to your prayers — yes and no.

THOUGHTS FOR FURTHER REFLECTION

"It is characteristic of the biblical God that he answers our prayers not always at the point of our request, but rather at the point of our needs, for God knows far better than we do what is best for us."

Ben Witherington III

"One must place oneself where one can hear God's word — whether on a mountaintop or in a church or synagogue."

Ben Witherington III

"Help me, God, to slow down, to be silent, so I can hear you and do your will and not mine."

Unknown

"Lord, teach me to listen. The times are noisy and my ears are weary with the thousand raucous sounds which continually assault them. Give me the spirit of the boy Samuel when he said to thee, 'Speak, for thy servant heareth.' Let me hear thee speaking in my heart. Let me get used to the sound of thy voice, that its tones may be familiar when the sounds of earth die away and the only sound will be the music of thy speaking Voice. Amen."

A. W. Tozer

"Talk to him in prayer of all your wants, your troubles, even of the weariness you feel in serving him. You cannot speak too freely, too trustfully, to him."

François Fénelon

"Chariot of Fire"
(Ezekiel 1)

- Worship God and reflect upon his power and majesty. Choose music to listen to or sing that praises God's faithful presence in your life.
- Read through Ezekiel 1 and the sermon once more. Reflect on how God has proven powerful, present, and faithful in your own life.
- Confess to God those times when you have doubted his power and faithfulness. Ask him to open your eyes to his presence in your own life.
- Journal through your thoughts on this passage and sermon. Visually represent the passage from Ezekiel or your thoughts from the sermon.

Write a poem, paint a picture, create a collage, write a song, or use another art form you enjoy to express yourself.

Thoughts for Further Reflection

"God is still a mighty and all-knowing and caring God, vitally concerned about our lives."

Ben Witherington III

"When suddenly God reveals his glory and sovereignty over the vicissitudes of life, even if it is a momentary glimpse of the larger design of things, one is never the same thereafter."

Ben Witherington III

"It is by prayer that we couple the powers of Heaven to our helplessness, the powers which can turn water into wine and remove mountains . . . the powers which can awaken those who sleep in sin and raise up the dead, the powers which can capture strongholds and make the impossible possible."

Ole Hallesby

"Transfixed"
(Revelation 21:1–22:5)

- Meditate on Revelation 21:1-5. Read through the passage slowly, taking in the details of John's vision of the new heaven and new earth. It may help to read through the passage several times. You might have someone read it to you so you may close your eyes and visualize the passage.
- Praise God for his promise of a new heaven and a new earth. Thank him for the opportunity to live this life for him. Praise him for his free gift of grace and for his faithfulness.
- Pray for strength to live a life of grace through faith. Pray for patience and perseverance in the everyday details of your life and work. Ask God to give you strength to live a full life for him. Pray also for eyes to see the

people around you that are crying out for God's grace and mercy. Ask the Lord to place people in your path with whom you might share his grace.

THOUGHTS FOR FURTHER REFLECTION

"Our ultimate destiny is to be fully conformed to the image of Christ by means of resurrection, and thereby made fit to dwell in the new Jerusalem, the holy city, in which there will be no more sin or suffering or sorrow or disease or decay or death or war or weapons or violence."

Ben Witherington III

"Our destiny is to be infinitely greater than our own poor selves."

Thomas Merton

"Nothing God has yet done for us can compare with all that is written in the sure word of prophecy. And nothing he has done or may yet do for us can compare with *what he is and will be to us!*"

A. W. Tozer

KINGDOM TIDE

The Dying of the Light

What in Creation?

Psalm 8

A sermon preached for the celebration of the safe return
of NASA Commander Robert Springer from the heavens

The Magnitude of Creator and Creation

It was to be an evening of fellowship over a game of bridge on a hot sum-
mer North Carolina night. The littlest member of the family had been put
to bed well in advance of the arrival of the guests, in her crib which she by
now had all but outgrown, as she was approaching four. The doorbell rang,
the guests arrived, and the adults got lost in the conviviality that invaded
their downstairs dining room — that is, until a severe thunderstorm
started rearing its ugly head over the city after a very hot and humid day.
The wind was suddenly gusting, the thunder rolled through in waves, and
lightning came crashing down in spectacular patterns. Suddenly the
mother's maternal alarm went off and she raced upstairs, worried that her
daughter would be frightened to death. She entered the nursery only to
find the little girl had pulled up the blinds all the way and was bouncing on
her mattress repeating over and over again, "Bang it again, God, bang it
again!"

Though it was perhaps three millennia prior to this little girl's encounter with creation, the person who wrote Psalm 8 seems to have felt
rather like she did when he contemplated the heavens. God has made a
vast, impressive, and in some ways stunningly beautiful world and universe. The power, design, complexity, majesty, and sheer size of creation is
so overwhelming at times that mere mortals like you and me can only
stand in wonder of it. Nothing that a human being has ever made can
come close to it, save perhaps another human life.

But our psalmist is not merely awestruck when he scans the skies, and, as we can see from this paean of praise, he is certainly not dumbstruck. Rather, he is inspired to speak in wonderful poetic verse, composing one of the great hymns in the Hebrew psalter. Notice that the first words that come out of his mouth are, "O God, our sovereign Lord, how majestic is your name in all the earth." Though it is not evident from the English translation, what the psalmist is claiming is that the God of Abraham, Isaac, and Jacob is not merely a nature deity associated with some particular part of nature or the cosmos, but is rather the Lord over it all. In effect, the psalmist says, "Everywhere I look I see your very fingerprints reflected in creation."

This idea of a single God who created the whole cosmos and whose nature is revealed in it all was a startling idea in 1000 B.C. and for some time thereafter. Other ancient near eastern peoples believed in gods, plural, and often saw them as part of nature or linked to one or another aspect of creation. Baal, for instance, so often mentioned in the Old Testament, was thought of as the god of storms, a rain god, whereas Shemesh was a sun god. Most ancients, it would appear, thought all beings, including the gods, were a part of the material universe, just as clearly as they thought that humans were fully under the sway of nature.

Sometimes this belief took the form of believing that the stars — imagined to be beings, the heavenly host, not mere inanimate matter — controlled human destinies. Not so our psalmist, who asserts that God has made it all and is over all. This God is no mere part of creation; rather, this God is the creator. This was to have momentous consequences for what may be called biblical faith. Among other things, it implied that the creation was not God, not divine. Therefore it might be examined and explored without irreverence. This "de-divinizing" of the cosmos in the Judeo-Christian tradition has rightly been said to be the underpinning of modern science. Science operates on the assumption that the universe is not defiled by inquiry; rather, it is there for our exploration, care, use. All of this arises out of the worldview articulated by our psalmist.

The cosmos, then, is God's handiwork, indeed God's artwork, something God created just as God created us. Creation is not divine in itself, nor is God contained by or a mere part of it. The measure of the psalmist's faith in God's sovereignty is made clear when he says quite literally that the sun, moon, and stars are the works of God's fingers. This means two things: 1) that in contrast to God, the universe is tiny, something God could shape with his fingers, metaphorically speaking, like a child might make something out of Play-Doh; and 2) that this magnificent creation came about without any great sweat on God's part. God is so powerful that one might say it was all in a week's work for this God. Friedrich Schiller, the great German poet, was right when he once said, "The universe is but a thought of God." What a thought that is!

The Minuteness of Creatures

When the psalmist contemplates the magnitude of God's creation, and thus the even greater magnitude of God, this leads him to consider himself and to reflect on the smallness and seeming impotence of human beings by comparison. The psalmist says that when he considers God's handi-work, he is led to ask, "What is a human being that you are mindful of us, or a child of humanity that you should care?"

The scientists tell us that a human being is halfway between the size of an atom and the size of a galaxy. Yet it is hardly surprising that when the psalmist becomes a stargazer he is struck by the minuteness of the human creature — so tiny in size, power, span of years. It reminds me of the prayer sometimes called the Seaman's Prayer: "O God, watch over me this day. The sea is so wide and my boat is so small." If God is such a majestic and gigantic being, then surely we must seem like ants to God. T. S. Eliot once put it this way: "O perpetual revolution of configured stars, O perpetual recurrence of determined seasons, . . . brings knowledge of motion but not of stillness; knowledge of speech, but not of silence; knowledge of words, but ignorance of the Word."

And yet our psalmist would not agree. Though the looking at cre-ation quite rightly makes us all feel small, this does not lead the psalmist to despair but rather to praising God's greatness, and furthermore to recog-nizing the great role and responsibility God has bequeathed to human be-ings. This is because he believes that we must not merely examine the book of nature but also the book of God to understand where human beings stand in the "pecking order" of creation.

The psalmist knows of human dignity, meaning, purpose because he has not merely scanned the skies, God's natural form of self-revelation, but has plumbed the depths of God's special revelation in Torah, his Word. In the very beginning of that Word we learn that we are created in God's very image or likeness, and thus the psalmist confidently asserts, "And yet you have made us but a little less than God." Our psalmist comes to creation already believing in God's Word, and thus he is able to see both God's majesty in creation and our role and purpose in relationship to it. He is convinced that believing, faith, trust leads to seeing things as they are and ought to be from God's perspective. This, of course, stands in contrast to some in the modern and postmodern era whose spiritual birth certificates are from Missouri, and so they shout, "Show me!" assuming only seeing leads to believing.

There was a Christian man dying of terminal cancer in the state of Washington who loved to go out and sit by his favorite stream and contemplate his favorite mountain range. One evening, feeling depressed that he would soon not be able to see these beautiful sights again, and rather frustrated that they would endure long after he was gone, something remarkable dawned on him. "I have been given the gift of eternal life — surely that should change my perspective on things!" It dawned on him how immediately that was the case, and so he shouted in triumph to the stream and the mountain "Long after you are gone, O stream, I will still exist. Long after you crumble into dust, O mountain, I will rise from the dust." It was something like this kind of faith that led the psalmist to say what he does about the place of humankind in relationship to a daunting universe that keeps rolling along for thousands and millions of years.

The Magnificent Domain Granted

The psalmist reassures us that we do not stand under the stars and the rest of creation, but rather in a real sense over them. They are there for us to explore, to appreciate, to wonder about, to rule over, for on a small scale we have been called to be mini-creators and mini-governors in the cosmos. It was not for nothing that God called upon humankind to fill the earth and subdue it, to tend the garden and care for it. The task of being governors and creators in the cosmos is a gift of God's grace to us. We have not earned it, we do not deserve it, and we often abuse the privilege. Nevertheless, it is our supernatural rather than our natural birthright. But with the birthright and power comes responsibility to properly exercise that power.

In our age of global warming and changing climate we have become all too painfully aware of how we have abused this right. We have polluted our skies, tainted our water supplies, destroyed our forests, fouled our coastlines with refuse and oil. The United States is at once the most abundantly blessed and most wasteful of all human societies to ever have existed upon the face of the earth. Though we are but 15% of earth's population, we consume something over 60% of the world's resources. We throw away enough food daily to feed most if not all of the rest of the world. Undoubtedly the psalmist would tell us we will be held accountable for how we have managed this beautiful planet hanging like a blue gem in a dark sky.

And yet our record is not merely a record of abuse, but also a record of the proper use of the knowledge, power, and dominion that God has granted us. Sometimes we have harnessed our energies and capacities for good, a shining example of which is the exploration of space as carried out in the life and work of Col. Robert Springer and astronauts and scientists like him. This quest to better understand the cosmos is essentially a noble one, for the better we understand the creation, the better we are likely to understand the mind of the Maker. If it is true that all truth is God's truth, then most certainly whenever and wherever the quest for knowledge leads to truth, it will also lead to God.

The great astronomer Robert Jastrow is reported to have once said words to the effect that when scientists have scaled the mountain of knowledge in seeking the origins of the universe, they will likely find on top of that mountain a theologian saying — "I told you so."

Credo for a Reverent but Curious Creature

It is part of the credo of both a person of biblical faith and of the scientist that we are to use what we learn from creation for the good of humanity, for the ordering of the world, for the caretaking of the environment. Of all the creatures on the earth only human beings, made "a little lower than God," are capable of pursuing such quests, however much we may also be unique in our ability to befoul our own nests.

Many of us need to recognize that science and religion should be working hand in hand as questers for knowledge about this world we are called upon to take care of. Some of us have forgotten that science and its child, technology, properly pursued, are good derivatives of a proper biblical understanding of creation, and of the mandate God has given us in relationship to it.

A warning is in order. Science without biblical faith can lead to nuclear holocaust, or medical technology without moral guidelines. But on the other hand biblical religion without science can lead to obscurantism and a failure to be open to the ever-new discoveries God would reveal to us about and through his creation by means of the hard work of scientists. Our psalmist did not believe there should be any bifurcation of truth, for all truth is the Creator's, for he has made it all, and truth at the end of the day must be seen from a holistic perspective, whether it is empirical or theological or moral truth we are referring to.

Sometimes the church has been a bit recalcitrant about moving in the direction God wants us to go when it comes to knowledge and truth. Toward the end of the nineteenth century there was a small Methodist church in Swan Quarter, North Carolina, near the coast. The church was a small white frame church set up on brick pile-ons on the corners of the building. For a long time the church had wanted to move to a little rise just outside of town, the only rise or hill in the entire area, but the property belonged to a Baptist who did not want to have any dealings with Methodists. After many overtures, the church finally gave up its quest for the land, but continued to pray. One day a hurricane rolled through this town near the coast of North Carolina, and the little church became an ark, floating down the main road out of town, and landing right on the rise that had so long been the bone of contention. Once the waters subsided, the Baptist, at first befuddled by this development, went to the county courthouse, got the deed notarized, and handed it over to the pastor of the Methodist church, with the comment, "God went to a lot of trouble to change my mind and get you that piece of land." Perhaps, we may hope, we are a bit more open-minded today to seeing God's hand in both his handiwork as well as his Word. But regardless of whether we are, the Bible is plain about the daunting task before us.

Our task is nothing less than the ordering of society for the good of all, nothing less than the conquering of all disease, all war, all hatred, all greed, all racism, all selfishness, all environmental mayhem — all of those things which are the enemies of life and life abundant. To this great task we have been called and have been equipped by God. I feel we may indeed repeat the words spoken by William Faulkner when he accepted the Nobel Prize: "I believe that in this human struggle, man will not merely endure, he will prevail."

I am not personally an optimist in the style of Norman Vincent

Peale, but I share my fellow southerner Faulkner's credo because I know that there was one man who walked the earth and did conquer disease, decay, and death, and suffering, sorrow, and sin. There was one man who walked this earth who truly offered the peace that passes understanding, the love that overcomes envy, jealousy, and hatred. There was one man who fed the multitude, perfectly exercised his God-given power and authority. There was one man now crowned with glory and honor, who walked this earth fully reflecting God's image, and who oddly enough called himself the Son of Man — the very same phrase used in this psalm to describe each one of us. It was no accident that those ancient astronomers, the Magi, were led to the cradle of this master. All truth is God's and ultimately leads to God.

But until God sees fit to consummate his plan for human history, his plan for creation and creature, we have a responsibility to take care of this earthly garden of which we are stewards, not owners. Until then, we must realize that God has made us curious and restless so we will find our rest, and our answers in God. Until then, we must learn and profit from the explorations of the universe by Col. Springer and many others. Until then, we must learn to sing with a good conscience — "O God, our Lord, how magnificent is thy name in all the cosmos."

Amen

The Supervising Shepherd
and the Heavenly Host

Psalm 23

The Way God Leads

Leaders come in many forms and fashions. Some are dictators, most are manipulators, some are governors, and some are even guardians of the people. When the psalmist wrote this beautiful song-poem he had a clear idea of whom he believed to be his leader, and this psalm is indeed a song of supreme trust and confidence in that Divine Leader. More than this, the psalmist is convinced he knows the role that God plays in his life — God, he says, is his shepherd, not a surprising image since this psalm, if by David as tradition maintains, was written by a former shepherd.

In other words, this image says something both about the psalmist's image of himself and his image of God. The term is relational in character. It is not just any God that the psalmist is talking about either — it is the biblical God, Yahweh. One could almost translate this first verse, "Because Yahweh is my shepherd, I shall not want."

What is the role of a shepherd? Put succinctly, it is to guide, guard, and goad the sheep. A shepherd is not one who does everything for the sheep, but he does what is necessary or essential. Too many human shepherds just assume that it is their task to do everything for the sheep they can do. But notice how the psalmist depicts the divine shepherd — he makes the sheep lie down in green pastures and he leads them beside still waters, but he neither makes them eat nor makes them drink. This they must do on their own: "You can lead a sheep to water. . . ." The shepherd is also the one who leads or guides them through the valleys of deep darkness where there is danger but nonetheless the sheep must follow his lead.

I once had a parishioner who was developmentally disabled. He was a sweet and very spiritual man in his mid-forties. He was always reading his Bible, and he especially loved Psalm 23. But he was puzzled. He came to me and asked, "Dr. Ben, it says that the Lord is my shepherd, I shall not want. But why does it say I shall not want? I want him, Dr. Ben — I need him." I was deeply touched by this simple question and the faith that stood behind it. I explained: "Ralph, it means that because God is your shepherd, you will lack for nothing essential." He smiled broadly and said, "I just knew it couldn't mean I wasn't supposed to want him." The psalmist has spoken with supreme confidence, and notice that he speaks about God being "my shepherd" in particular — this is a personal matter. But more profoundly, we must follow God if God is to truly be our shepherd.

Sheep are not notably bright, but they do know how to play follow the leader. Dale Carnegie told of the days when he was growing up on a sheep farm. He used to love to watch when the sheepdog would herd the sheep into their pen at the end of the day. He would open the gate and then stick a long stick in the entrance way. The dog would jump over the stick, followed by the first sheep, and so on. But halfway through the process, Carnegie would pull the stick out of the gateway to see what happened. Sure enough, the sheep just kept jumping over a now-imaginary stick in the gateway. Such creatures need good leadership, and the psalmist counts himself among them!

Notice that the psalmist does not think that life is all hearts and flowers. His faith and trust is simple, but not naïve. The reference to "still waters" is important because sheep are likely to fall in and drown if taken to a place where there is rapidly running water. Furthermore, the text speaks of being led through the valley of the shadow. The text may be translated as either "shadow of deep darkness" or "shadow of death." Either way, the image is of a dangerous passage. Imagine a deep ravine with a dry river bed, with wolves and other wild animals lurking on the hills as the light fades.

Hear how the psalmist responds to the trial of having to go through such a place in life. He says, "I will fear no evil." He does not say, "There is no evil." He knows there is evil that can harm and even kill. He is walking by faith rather than fear because of the next line: "For you are with me." It is not the smallness of the difficulty but the greatness of his God that gives the psalmist this ability to pass through such places. John Wesley, as he lay on his deathbed, kept repeating a single phrase as he passed on into eternity — "Best of all, God is with me." The psalmist would have heartily agreed. Even on the voyage through death, God is with us.

This shepherd is not merely capable of leading and comforting and caring; he is also capable of correction. Scholars tell us that Palestinian shepherds, both in antiquity and today, carry two implements with them — a club or rod to beat off the wild animals, and a shepherd's crook to guide and goad, to discipline, and even to extract with the hook a sheep that has fallen in a hole. It is striking that the psalmist draws comfort from both the tool of protection but also the instrument of correction and rescue. The psalmist draws solace from the fact that God loves him enough to do both things for him.

The psalmist goes on to stress that God leads him in the right paths — or we could translate it, "the paths of righteousness." Either way, it is interesting that it is not said to be done just for the psalmist's benefit. The text says, "for his name's sake." God has a stake in our lives, and God's honor is affected by how we behave or live our lives precisely because people will look at us and evaluate God on the basis of what they see in us. It is to God's own credit and benefit to properly lead the sheep. He wants them to reflect his own glory and nature and wisdom.

Sometimes this psalm has been seen as akin to the well-known poem called "Desiderata" — "Go placidly amongst the noise and haste. . . ." In fact, we have the very oriental rendering of this psalm by Toki Miyashina, which begins:

> The Lord is my pacesetter
> I shall not rush.
> He makes me stop and rest for quiet intervals.
> He provides me with images of stillness,
> which restore my serenity.
> He leads me in ways of efficiency through
> calmness of mind, and his guidance is peace.

As beautiful as this is, it is only in a small way on target when it comes to the original intent of the psalmist. The goal was not to lead the sheep to a placid place, but to a place of nourishment. It is not the serenity of the sheep, but their very life force that is referred to in saying, "He restores my soul." Further, as we shall see, the images of hospitality have to do with fellowship with God and even with enemies, not primarily with the replenishing of the mind or giving us inner peace. Yes, God is the psalmist's pacesetter and leader, but he is leading him on an arduous journey, and even the last line is probably about journeying, as we shall see.

The Way God Feeds

The imagery of the psalm changes dramatically in verses 5 and 6. We are now in the tent of the itinerant shepherd. Here he is seen as the host, one who literally feeds the under-shepherd, the psalmist, who is now seen as the guest rather than as the sheep. A shepherd would often host guests in his tent made of camel's hair, and we can still see this tradition alive today with the Bedouin, who still sojourn in the Holy Land, often in the wilderness near Jericho. The custom of the age in regard to hospitality was that if one welcomed someone into one's tent, then one was obliged to treat that person as a guest and a friend, even if in fact they were an enemy. Nothing was to spoil the hospitable moment. The phrase "in the presence of my enemies" may simply mean they are outside the tent and the host will protect from their attack since the psalmist is his guest, or it may go further and suggest that the enemies have also been invited to dine. Could it be to bring about reconciliation?

Here is a magnificent feast at which the host has anointed the guest on the head with olive oil, a common custom on such occasions since the guest was coming off the hot and dusty road and his scalp would have been dry and cracked from the beating sun. We hear as well of the cup being filled repeatedly to overflowing. This host has endless resources. The psalmist thinks of the larger implications of the way God provides for him and adds that surely God's goodness and lovingkindness will chase him down, follow him, trail along behind him all the days of his life. If it is God who leads and feeds you, you will lack for nothing essential throughout life, says the psalmist, especially when it comes to God's goodness and mercy or lovingkindness.

The only appropriate response to such a gracious host and shepherd is what we find in the final phrase of the psalm — "And I will return to [it could also be translated 'dwell in'] the house of the Lord over and over, or for as long as I live!" It is in the house of the Lord that the psalmist can worship God truly and show his gratitude for God's provision. It is in God's presence that he could always find joy, strength, provision, guidance. The question is, should we not be like this psalmist and follow the path he trod? The psalmist begins his pilgrimage in the pastures; he ends in the Temple. Such is the haven and destination of all God's sheep. It is not a surprise that Jesus called himself the Good Shepherd. In so doing he was identifying with Yahweh in this psalm and saying that he fulfilled these functions for his followers.

I will leave you with a final sheep story. Some years ago I was driving through the Lake District in England with my parents, who were visiting. My mother was a nervous wreck because she was sure I was going to hit something, as it was a one-lane road with many turns and twists and hills. Suddenly, we came over a hill and there was a whole herd of sheep standing in the middle of the road. They did not budge an inch and I had to quickly put on the brakes, narrowly missing a collision with the front two sheep. They stood there staring at my car, never budging. You could almost hear the conversation between those two sheep. "Well, Heathcliff, do you reckon we should move?" "I don't see why we need to, Gertie, I mean the thing has stopped racing at us." They never flinched. The shepherd and the sheepdog came along and suddenly they were all in motion and quickly out of the lane. Sheep are not notably bright, but they do know how to play follow the leader. Perhaps this is the most important reason why the psalmist is suggesting that we should go and do likewise.

Amen

Attempting to Overcome a Tempting

1 Corinthians 10:1-13

God and Tempting

One of the first things one learns in the Christian pilgrimage is how different human beings are from God. God has always been. Humans live and die. God knows all things. Human knowledge is limited. God is and can be everywhere at once both in time and outside of time. Human beings are finite. God is all-powerful. Human power is decidedly limited. God is spirit and invisible. Humans are flesh and all too visible. Paul stresses one more major difference: while all human beings have sinned and fallen short of God's glory, God never has and never does sin. All that God desires and does is good. There is nothing evil, wicked, or even questionable in God's character. As the prophet says, "God is light, and in him is no darkness at all." There is not even a shadow of turning in God. God, then, is holy and pure, whereas Satan is the opposite of this, and is on occasion called the tempter (1 Thess. 3:5; Matt. 4:3).

The author of James puts the matter directly: "Let no one say, when he is tempted, 'I am tempted by God,' for God cannot be tempted by evil, and he himself tempts no one" (1:13). Why, then, does it say in the Lord's Prayer, "Lead us not into temptation"? Well, as it turns out the Greek word *periasmos* can refer to either a tempting or a testing. It is an old theological distinction, but a valuable one: that God tests us, seeking to strengthen our character, but the Devil tempts us, trying to destroy our character. In fact, the prayer should probably be translated, "Do not put us to the test, but rather deliver us from the Evil One." This saying reminds us of Jesus' own experience with temptation and perhaps Job's as well. A test, then, can be seen as a positive experience even if on occasion we may pray to avoid it. A temptation, however, always tries to allure or entice someone to do something which is sinful or evil. No temptation is properly so called unless we are at least slightly inclined to do the prohibited action. If someone prohibited me from eating liver, I can honestly say I would never struggle with the temptation to violate that prohibition. But this leads us to talk about human beings and our temptations little and large.

Human Beings and Temptation

Here we are on more familiar ground, for all of us at some juncture have both been tempted and been the source of temptation, whether wittingly or unwittingly. Consider the following example. Under the windshield wiper of his car, a driver stuck a note. It read, "I've been circling this block for twenty minutes. I am late for an appointment and if I don't park here I'll miss a job interview — 'forgive us our trespasses.'" When the man returned to his car he found an envelope with a note from an officer which read, "I've circled this block for twenty years, and if I don't give you a ticket I'll lose my job — 'lead us not into temptation.'"

But I have an even better example. I once had a parishioner who was a new Christian. He was a good fellow but he did not know his Bible well and he was worried about falling prey to violating the Bible unwittingly. One day he called me and asked if the Bible prohibited breeding hunting dogs because his fellow Christian carpenter had told him the Bible forbade such an activity. I had never heard of such a thing, but I promised I would look up all the references to dogs in the Bible and get back to him. There was nothing in the New Testament of relevance, but there was a verse in the Old Testament that read in the King James Version words to the effect of, "Thou shalt not breed with the dogs." I called up my parishioner and told him I had good news and bad news. "Give me the good news first," he said. "Well, there is no problem with you breeding little furry four-footed creatures who wag their tails." "What's the bad news, then?" he asked. I said, "Well, there is this Old Testament verse that says you shouldn't have children with foreign women if you are a true Jew." There was a pregnant pause at the other end of the line and then he said, "Well, I am feeling so much better now, pastor, as that will be no temptation for me, and besides, my wife Betty Sue is just from the next county, Chatham County."

We have all been tempted, and we have all been tempters at one time or another. Oscar Wilde, a man of great wit, was once offered some bonbons while at a party in London. The waitress said, "Can I tempt you with bonbons?" Wilde quipped, "Madam, I can resist anything but temptation." But did you realize you can even put God to the test?

Are you not testing God when you indirectly or directly say to God, "Okay, bless me, heal me, prove you are real." We can also put God to the test when we deliberately keep sinning even after we have given our life to Christ. We must beware of acting in this fashion, as even a moment's reflection on the Cross will suggest. But perhaps you have come to the place in your life where you feel like sin is inevitable as temptation seems to be making you an offer you can't refuse. Is this really the case for the Christian? Let us reflect for a moment on our text for today.

Christians and Temptation

Hear first the good news. As Shakespeare once said, "It is one thing to be tempted, another thing to fall." Being tempted is not the same as sinning. A wise minister once said, "Temptation is the tempter looking through the keyhole of your heart. Sin is drawing back the latch bolt and allowing him to enter." Christians should not be surprised or dismayed about temptations. In fact, Christians should especially expect them since they are not already on the side of the powers of darkness. Christians are usually more sensitive to what a temptation is, but they cannot be said to be inherently more vulnerable to temptation, precisely because he who is in us is greater than any temptation.

Here is where I stress that Paul says in 1 Corinthians 10 that no temptation has overcome a Christian that is not common to humanity or beyond our power to endure; with any temptation God can provide an adequate means of escape. Here is a scriptural promise worth claiming! We should pray for deliverance, pray "Deliver us from the Evil One!" in such a situation — and God will act and strengthen the person in question.

This is not to say that Christians just by trying hard or having enough will power can resist temptation. It is only by God's grace and Spirit that we are upheld in such situations. Without God's help we could and will fail and fall. But again the promise is sure — *no temptation* need ever overwhelm us. But there is another point of importance. God's provision often comes in the hour of need, and not before.

Corrie ten Boom tells the story of her worry as a young woman about what she would say if Nazis came to her house in Holland, where her family was harboring Jews. She spoke with her wise father about this, and he asked her a question. "Corrie, when do I give you the ticket for the train? Weeks before we depart, or right before we get on the train?" Corrie answered, "Obviously, Papa, it is right before I get on the train so I will use it properly and not lose the ticket." "So it will be when the Nazis come, if you are called to speak to them. God will give you the words, and help you resist the temptation to say or do something wrong."

We should never try to guess in advance what our strength will be in the hour of trial, for God will provide in such a time as that, like God provided Abraham the ram at the very last moment when he was about to sacrifice Isaac. Furthermore, it is not just the temptation that causes sin. An internal process is involved; as James says, "Each person is tempted when he is lured and enticed by his own desire, and then desire when it conceives, gives birth to sin" (1:14-15). If the temptation does not take root, and we have a choice about that (not always a choice about whether or when we will be tempted) we have won the battle. The point is just this — such deliberate capitulation to temptation and sin in the Christian life is not inevitable. We have the presence of Christ and the Spirit with us and so we can win this running battle, one skirmish at a time.

Victory over Temptation

How, then, shall we have victory over temptation? There are many remedies, one of which is simply to get as far away as we can from the source of temptation, to flee and not leave a forwarding address.

John Wesley used to advise that individuals involve themselves so deeply in God's work and in performing good works that they would have no time for temptation. This was based on the old saying that "idle hands are the Devil's playground," and there is more truth than poetry to that in a culture in which we have, or try to have, so much leisure time for all sorts of non-essential activities. I would simply say that prayer, fasting, Bible study, good fellowship, and family activities are all things that help us avoid temptation. As we can see temptation is a huge subject and there is no end of evidence and examples to consider, not least because humans are so good at succumbing to it. But I would simply leave you with this thought: God is greater than the scope of our sin or our temptations. His power is greater than that of the nefarious one, and we can indeed claim the great promise in our text for today about the ability to resist temptation. In him we shall have the victory.

Amen

We Haven't Got a Prayer

Luke 11:1; Matthew 6:5-13

What Is Prayer?

Tonight we need to wrestle with some very basic questions: What is prayer? Why bother to pray? How should we pray? But it will be best if we start with a simple definition of prayer. Prayer is, of course, conversing with God, or beseeching God, or complaining to God, or interceding for someone with God, or praising and thanking God. In all these forms of prayer God is the object and we are the supplicants, which implies that we recognize that God is God, and we are not. George Herbert, in a wonderful poem, portrays prayer as "God's breath in man returning to its birth," and "the soul in paraphrase," and "the heart in pilgrimage." We will return to these images in a moment, but I would suggest first that there is something to be learned by some of the ways people talk about prayer.

I have an old radio that broke down not too long ago, and I brought it to a repair shop to have it fixed. After a few days I stopped by the shop and asked the man at the counter whether it was ready. He said, "No, but we'll hope and pray it will be ready next week." What did he mean? Well, he probably meant two things: 1) that there was an element of uncertainty about whether my radio would be ready then, but he desired or hoped that it would be; 2) by "pray" he indicated not only his desire, but also that in part it was out of his hands — he could not control the circumstances that would determine whether it would be ready then. "Pray," then, indicated desire but also a lack of control. It has been said many times that our heart's desire is our real prayer, whatever our lives may say. So Herbert was right —

real prayer is the heart in pilgrimage. It entails the recognition that we do not have the object of our desire and cannot by sheer will power obtain it.

Another common phrase we hear is, "He hasn't got a prayer." By this we mean that the person in question has no hope of fulfilling some sort of plan or effort. There is a strong element of hope in prayer, this colloquial phrase suggests. But for the Christian it is not just a matter of wishful thinking. There is a basis for the hope.

We can also learn a great deal about prayer from the traditional gestures and postures associated with prayer. No doubt many of you have seen the great woodcut, or a painting of it, by Albrecht Dürer of the great gnarled hands. They are pressed together in a gesture of supplication that actually goes back to the days in which a servant beseeching his master would put his folded hands between the master's own hands. The gesture pointed towards heaven, of course, indicates a heavenly Master. Prayer is practically synonymous with supplication of some kind. "Lord, help me. . . ." There is certainly nothing wrong and everything natural about this sort of prayer, but it would be wrong to only go to God as a court of last resort. Prayer is not just a safety valve or an extra parachute when one's life is in free fall, and God is not just the Father we call on when we need to be bailed out.

Prayer is as well an act of submission. It is a way to say to the Lord, "Thy will be done." It is putting all matters, not just important matters, into his hands. It is a recognition of who we are as creatures and who God is as creator, savior, Lord. This is why the gestures of bowing the head or closing the eyes are so appropriate. Prayer is an act of humbling ourselves before our Maker, recognizing that he is in control, and we turn to God not only for help but because we are answerable to God as his creatures.

Why Pray?

But now we come to a harder question — why bother to pray, especially in light of what the Bible says about God's omniscience (see Psalm 139:1-8, for example)? What do you say to someone who already knows everything before you say it? More to the point, why bother if God knows us better than we know ourselves and our wants? Clearly we do not pray to inform God about anything, but we may well pray to inform ourselves about God's will for us, as Jesus did in the Garden of Gethsemane.

A second bothersome question is this: Can we actually twist God's arm by praying, perhaps praying fervently? Is prayer really, as George Herbert put it, "reversed thunder, Christ's side piercing spear," whereby we can wrestle a blessing from the Almighty? The answer to this is surely no, unless we are already praying according to God's will. We certainly cannot force God to violate his own nature or will in order to fulfill or indulge ours. God is not some cosmic bellhop or genie whose job in life is to say, "Your wish is my command!" But prayer that accords with God's will availeth much.

There are at least four good reasons to pray, and they all start with the letter C — communion, confession, cooperation, communication of concern. Firstly, then, we pray in order to be personal with God, to develop a personal relationship, to draw close to our Maker. It is a means not merely of making contact but of establishing intimacy with our Abba. From a theological point of view, we are able to do this because Christ has reconciled us to God and made such communication possible and fruitful, so we may be in fellowship with God. And we should never be embarrassed to pray, even in public.

A Christian farmer was spending the day in a nearby large city. Entering a restaurant at noon, he found a table near a group of young men. When his meal was served, he quietly bowed his head and gave thanks for the food before him. Observing this, the young men thought they would ridicule and embarrass the man. One called out in a loud voice, "Hey hillbilly, does everyone do that where you live?" Looking the rude youth straight in the face, the old man said calmly: "No, son, the pigs don't."

As for communion with God, we have close communion with the Father precisely because the Son has such communion and he has given us the access as a free and gracious gift. We "come to the Father through Jesus the Son," as the old hymn says. Notice how Jesus taught his disciples to pray to God as he did — calling God "Abba." Romans 8:14-16 says, "For all who are led by the Spirit of God are sons of God. When we cry 'Abba, Father!' it is the Spirit himself bearing witness with our spirit that we are children of God." Thus we pray to have this "mystic sweet communion with God the three in One." We can be truly personal with God, in the same fashion that Jesus was.

We also pray prayers of confession. This is necessary so we may be open with God about our sin. Of course, we are not telling God anything he does not know, but it forces us to humble ourselves and does not allow us to hide anything from God or from ourselves. Confession to God prevents a person from deceiving themselves and living a lie. Obviously, confession is a hard sort of prayer to pray, especially if one is a proud person and has trouble admitting mistakes or sins. To admit to someone you love that you have sinned against them or done wrong is to admit failure to the one before whom one wants to appear in the best possible light. It is hard work.

Perhaps the most exciting thing about prayer is the third of the four C's — it allows us to participate in God's powerful plan to change the world. This is the C of cooperation. Many people will tell you prayer is powerful, but in fact prayer is not a talisman or charm. Prayer in itself is not like rubbing a magic lantern. It does not work automatically, or if you just get the words just right. For example, it is no good to petition your professors for good grades! It won't help, no matter how much you are in earnest. Prayer only works because we have a powerful God who loves us and longs to help, and longs to enlist us in his plan and service to reclaim his world. If we pray according to God's will, we may expect results. But we must bear in mind that while God answers all prayers, even no is an answer to prayer, though it might not be the one we want. Furthermore, "Yes, but not now" is also an answer to prayer. My point is that God answers all prayers in his own way, in his own time, according to his own will, not ours. We cannot make God an offer he can't refuse by praying, however pious we may be.

Of course prayers of intercession, prayers of communication of concern, whether interceding for others or self, are perhaps the most frequently mentioned kinds of prayer. We are a needy people, and so this is no surprise. The joy of all this is that God even uses the most feeble of prayers for his ends, and it is a great and holy privilege to be partners with the Almighty in changing human lives.

One of the greatest men of prayer in any century was George Mueller of Bristol, England. He was once asked by a clergyman, a Dr. Pierson, if he had ever prayed a prayer that had not been answered. Mueller thought for a moment and responded, "Sixty-two years, 3 months, 5 days, and 2 hours have passed since I began to pray for two men that they might be converted. I have prayed daily for them ever since and as yet neither of them shows any signs of turning to God." Dr. Pierson then asked, "Do you still expect God to convert them?" "Certainly," was the confident reply. "Do you think God would lay on his child such a burden for 62 years if he had no purpose for their conversion?"

Not long after Mr. Mueller's death, Dr. Pierson was again in Bristol preaching. In the course of his sermon he mentioned this conversation. As he was leaving at the end of the service a woman came up to him and told him, "One of those two men was my uncle, and he was converted and died a few weeks ago." Pierson was later to learn that the other man was brought to Christ in Dublin, Ireland, thereafter.

How Should We Pray?

Like the disciples in Luke 11:1, we need to be taught how to pray, and the Lord's prayer is a model prayer, letting us know the kind of things we ought to be praying about. Sometimes our very nature resists praying and we need this sort of prompting or guide, and sometimes we just don't know what to pray for. But what is most striking about this prayer is that before one ever arrives at petitions one is first urged to hallow God's name, to praise God. Adoration is to precede either confession or petition or even thanksgiving prayers. In other words, the first function and order of prayer is worshiping God, aligning ourselves in right relationship with God.

Prayer should be offered in the context of adoration; it should focus on necessary things, as the Lord's prayer suggests, even something as simple as daily bread, or power to resist temptations, and just as it should begin with the intimacy of addressing God as Abba, it should end "in Jesus' name," for Jesus is interceding for us in heaven. He pleads our causes and cases, and the Father listens to the Son. But of course we must ask: Is the prayer I am praying something Jesus would pray, should I really sign his name to this prayer, and would he do so? When we pray in Jesus' name, it is asking his help, endorsement, approval, power for our prayer.

Prayer is indeed, as Herbert said, the soul in paraphrase, and God's breath in us returning to its source. So call any time day or night. There will be no static on the line, and no need to say, "Can you hear me now?" You need not wait until the weekend rates, as there are no rates at all. You can dial direct without ministerial assistance, without calling "parson to parson," the line is never busy, you can talk as long as you like, and best of all — God will always be at home listening.

Amen

Taxing Situations and
Insufferable Self-Centeredness

Luke 18:9-14

O for a Faith That Will Not Shrink

It has been said many times that human beings have an infinite capacity for self-justification, even when confronted with their own sin or shortcomings in a clear way. The story is told about a man who was shopping in a mall and took a shirt to the counter asking for an explanation for the label in the shirt. "It says 'shrink-resistant,' but what really does that mean?" asked the man. The lady at the counter thought for a moment and replied, "It means it does not want to shrink, but it probably will anyway." Is that the way it is with us when we are confronted with our real selves — not just the personas we project? Is our self-honesty merely shrink-resistant, or are we really prepared to own up to what we are actually like? Instead of engaging in self-justification, or even trying to justify ourselves before God, can we simply accept that real justification is a gift from God, and it is a gift we can only receive if we are both repentant and painfully honest with God about our real condition and who we really are? These are the sorts of questions we must explore in our sermon text for today — the parable of the Pharisee and the tax collector.

This parable makes a fitting finale to the Gospel of Luke's central section, or travel account. This is because it makes perfectly clear what Luke thinks is the proper attitude with which any human being should approach God. As with the immediately preceding parable of the widow and the unjust judge, there are two contrasting principal figures involved, one whom Luke wants his audience to emulate and one whose example they should avoid. The setting of this parable is the Temple itself, where both men have gone, perhaps during the hours for public prayer (9 a.m. and 3 p.m.) or perhaps at another time to pray privately. Not stopping in the Court of the Gentiles, they would have gone straight into the Court of Israel, where Jews were permitted to pray. But what very different prayers and prayer postures these two men assume!

I Have Seen the Pharisee . . .

It needs to be stressed from the outset that the Pharisee's shortcoming is of course *not* that he has avoided sin, or that he has performed various good deeds and religious duties in exemplary fashion. He has been legally and ritually pure, he has fasted and tithed in a noteworthy fashion. Nor is this Pharisee being hypocritical — he really *is* thankful he has not lived like the tax collector. But notice the number of times the word "I" comes up in his prayer. In fact, verse 11 says that he "prayed about himself" — about his own accomplishments! The irony is that he has not been like the tax collector either in a good or a bad sense. He has not seen his need for God, his need for grace and mercy. Notice, however, that he not only avoids serious sin, and fasts twice a week, he also does more than the Law requires in that he tithes out of everything he gets, not just out of his earnings. These are all good things, but they do not allow one to establish a claim on God.

The problem with the Pharisee seems comprised of three factors: 1) that he evaluates himself by comparing himself to others rather than measuring himself simply by the divine standard; 2) that he judges others by how things appear to him, which is to say on a superficial and external basis. He does not know the heart of the tax collector; and 3) he is both self-centered and believes that the basis of his self-esteem is and should be what he has accomplished as a religious person. He has no real sense of his own sinfulness and unworthiness before God, and therefore he cannot understand God's grace. He has not seen that he cannot justify himself, he can only receive such a status as a gift from God, as the tax collector does. He exhibits neither humility toward God nor compassion for his neighbor, nor any capacity for realizing his own shortcomings.

As Luke says of such a Pharisee in verse 9, providing the interpretation of this character in advance, "They trusted in themselves that they were righteous" — or it could be translated, "They trusted in themselves because they were righteous," which seems quite possible here. The Pharisee is neither a hypocrite nor a wicked person, but he does indeed rely on his own performance as a basis to evaluate himself and, so to speak, "make God an offer he can't refuse." Now it seems to me that this is a fault many of us can identify with and regularly are guilty of. We judge ourselves by what we do, and we think somehow in our heart of hearts that God will just have to accept us if we do all these good things — like being honest on the job, or supporting our family, or tithing at our church. But while we in our self-talk are busily giving kudos to ourselves, by comparing ourselves to others and assuming God must surely approve all these good things we do, we are forgetting some very fundamental truths about how we receive right-standing or justification in the eyes of God.

Now the Tax Collector Did Not Even Look Up . . .

How very different are the demeanor, body language, and words of the tax collector! Notice that he also is a Jew, but he is a Jew in a despised profession, collecting taxes or tolls for the Romans. He would be viewed as something of a traitor in Judea. While the Pharisee assumed the usual posture of standing and praying, perhaps with uplifted hands, the tax collector, according to verse 13, stood at a distance, would not even look up to heaven, beat his breast, and simply said, "God, have mercy upon me, a sinner." We may compare this verse with the ancient extrabiblical book *1 Enoch* 13:5, which says of the fallen angels referred to in Genesis 6, "They did not raise their eyes to heaven out of shame for their sins." The sense of remorse and repentance for sin seems very evident in the case of the tax collector. The tax collector offers God no list of virtues (unlike the Pharisee), nor a list of excuses, but rather just a frank recognition that he has sinned and an appeal for mercy. Jesus ends the story with the pointed remark that "this man went away justified rather than the other." The second half of the verse provides the reason this is so — all those who exalt themselves will be humbled and the converse of that remark is also true. Once again, the Lukan theme of eschatological reversal comes to the fore.

While it has sometimes been said that Jesus did not teach the idea of "justification by grace through faith," that being seen as a Pauline creation, this parable surely makes clear that he taught some variant of this idea. It is a caricature of early Judaism to say it had no concept of grace and the forgiveness of God as a necessary component of God's relationship with his people. To the contrary, Jesus and other early Jewish sages make clear that this was not so. Indeed, the Hebrew Scriptures themselves make this clear at various junctures (see, for example, Isaiah 63:4-9; Psalm 116 on God hearing a cry for mercy; and Hosea 11:1-11). In fact, as Fred Craddock says, this picture of the compassionate and merciful God is "as old as the Garden of Eden, the tower of Babel, and Jonah's mission to Nineveh."

Notice that Jesus and Luke have not chosen to contrast a Jew with a non-Jew in this passage, but rather the story has contrasted one Jew with another. This story should never have led to anti-Semitic notions. It simply shows the strength of a form of Jewish religion that it could be self-critical of its shortcomings and of its least exemplary exponents. Any religion should be judged at its best, not its worst, and on the basis of its best practitioners, not its worst. But what should we as Christians derive from this story, other than the need to avoid caricaturing any particular devout Jewish or Christian group, ancient or modern, as all hypocritical Pharisees?

Who Are We More Like in This Parable?

Look again at how Luke frames this parable at its outset — who is it for? It is for those who "trusted in themselves that they were righteous and regarded others with contempt." Could this ever describe us? Consider for a moment that this Pharisee might well be an outstanding member of any church, if we are judging by his religious behavior. Who doesn't want a fellow church member that tithes, that prays fervently and earnestly, that avoids sin! Doubtless this Pharisee was genuinely glad he was not like the despised tax collector! Have you never felt that way? Have you never prayed to God and said, thank you, Lord, that I am not like this or that person, that I am not in the pickle that this or that person is in because of their deeds? Have you never given way to the temptation to pick yourself up by putting others down? If there is even a hint of this in you, you are more like the Pharisee in this parable than you realize.

But the real bottom line in this parable is whether you ultimately trust in yourself and your own self-evaluation, or whether you trust in God and his grace. If you are playing to an audience of one, is that one yourself and your own self-evaluation, or is it God? When you pray, do you go into God's presence with a list of positive things you have done, as though God might overlook them and fail to give you the brownie points you deserve? Or have you realized that while your faith and trust might be shrink-resistant, it is not shrink-proof, and in fact it is too much focused on your trust in yourself and your own evaluation of yourself rather than your trust in God?

You can say this about the tax collector — he knew his need for God, he knew he had no sufficient basis to make a claim on God, he knew he was a sinner, and he knew he had to just throw himself on the mercy of God. And in doing that, he went away justified. He was justified, set right in his relationship with God, by the Almighty, not by the voice of his own conscience. Since the truth is that we all sin and fall short of God's highest and best for us, should we ever come into the presence of God like the Pharisee in this parable, or is it more in line with self-effacing honesty that we approach the throne as a supplicant, not a claimant — more like the tax collector? Do we even know where we are going, or how to get there, when it comes to our relationship with God? Do we understand that right standing with God comes when we admit we are lost and don't know where we are going and ask for God's pardon and guidance?

Albert Einstein was a man so caught up in the life of the mind that he was frequently forgetful about ordinary, everyday things. My Bible professor from UNC, Dr. Bernard Boyd, used to tell stories about meeting the great man in downtown Princeton many years ago and Einstein would have a grocery or to-do list safety-pinned to the front of his sweater so he would remember what he came to town to do. Another story of a similar ilk is told about Einstein when he was taking a train trip. The conductor came along to collect the tickets and Einstein was fumbling through his effects and pockets and briefcase looking everywhere for the ticket. He couldn't find it. The conductor had recognized that it was Einstein and said, "It's alright, Mr. Einstein, I trust you. I am sure you bought a ticket." Yet still Einstein kept frantically searching for the ticket, getting down on his knees and looking under the seat. The conductor came back a few minutes later and saw this improbable charade, and told Einstein again, "It's all right, sir, we don't need to find the ticket, I know who you are." Einstein replied: "You don't understand, young man; I also know who I am, but I don't know where I am going!"

The Pharisee in our text for today was both quite confident he knew who he was and where he was going in life but he was wrong about both. By contrast, the tax collector had only of late come to a realization of who he really was, and he also knew he was lost. Fortunately, he had enough sense to humble himself and go to the One who could remedy that problem — God. In the end, it's better to admit you are lost so that Jesus will say of you, "That person went away justified, and not the other."

Amen

From Image to Likeness

1 John 3:2

A Lasting Impression

Have you ever watched someone use a seal and sealing wax? The hot wax is poured on the envelope and then the signet ring or seal is pressed into the wax, leaving a very close replica of the design of the seal or signet ring in the wax. Now, of course, the impression left in the wax is not the same as the original. For one thing, it is an "impression," whereas the protruding features of the seal are, strictly speaking, an "expression" with raised images and letters. Nevertheless, there is a close resemblance between the seal and the impression it leaves. When the Bible talks about human beings created in the image of God, this sort of analogy is often brought up, but what does it really mean to be created in God's image? The seal leaves a physical impression and there is a physical resemblance between the impression and the seal, but surely this is not what the Bible is talking about. We need to ask a different set of questions.

What is it that distinguishes us from all other sentient beings? According to Genesis 1–2, it is that we are created in the image of God. But what, really, does that mean? It certainly does not mean that we look like God. It has nothing to do with physical appearance. God the first person of the Trinity is spirit, and so has no physical form. We might be prone to think physical form is meant (and indeed this is the Mormon interpretation of the matter), not least because we have commercials inundating us with the slogan, "Image is everything," referring to outward and visible form. But we must not allow popular culture to dictate how we think about the biblical concept of image.

Perhaps a clue is found in the words from heaven in the Genesis account — "Let us make human beings in our image, and after our likeness." Who is the "us" here? Jewish commentators speculated that it was God and his heavenly retinue, the angels, whereas the Church Fathers felt sure that members of the Trinity were conversing with each other. In either case, the issue becomes what "image" means if it is something God could share with others, including with us?

One theory has been that "image" refers to our mental capacities. But in view of the frequently irrational, not to mention immoral nature of human conduct, there is reason to doubt this is what the author of Genesis had in mind. Humans are the only creatures who foul their own nests, and frequently animals seem to act in a more rational and "humane" manner than people. Consider, for example, the unconditional love a dog often gives its master.

Another theory is that the reference to being in God's image is in regard to free will. But does this really distinguish human beings from at least the higher primates, and indeed many other creatures? Do they not also have wills, and make choices, at least on occasion? It would seem they do. What is it that distinguishes humans from the lower order of creatures? I would suggest that it is our capacity for relationship with God, a personal relationship that goes beyond the relationship other creatures could have with God. And with this privilege comes great responsibility.

Iconoclasm — the Destruction of the Image

The story of creation is only the beginning of the human drama. It is rapidly followed by the story of human sin and the Fall. It becomes a story of a violated, even a broken relationship with God. The image of God in human beings had been marred or distorted by sin.

It was like looking at one's image in a broken mirror: though the image was still present, and recognizably so, it was distorted, broken. There arose a difference, indeed a gap, between image and likeness. Though created in the image of God, we were not at all acting like God. The human pilgrimage became a journey from broken image to likeness. But this journey was not one human beings could make on their own, or even with mere mortal help. Someone had to go this road before us, and for us — and that someone was Jesus, for whom there was not a gap or division between being image of God, and being in God's likeness. He alone was a person who could say, "Whoever has seen me has seen my Father." After Jesus, the human pilgrimage had to go through Jesus, in order to achieve the likeness of God.

1 John 3:2 puts it this way: "Beloved, we are God's children now; it does not yet appear what we shall be, but we know that when he appears we shall be like him." Notice both what is said here and what is implied. It is implied that, even though we are Christians and so God's children, we are not yet like him, for we have not yet been fully conformed to the image of Christ. This only happens when he appears and we assume the same resurrection existence that Christ assumed at Easter. Only then will we be fully and truly like him. We are already God's children, but we will become like him in the future. Notice the all important word "like" — we do not become God. We only become like our Maker, like Jesus himself. There is a big difference. The New Testament does not ever affirm that the Creator-creature distinction will be obliterated — not even in the sweet by-and-by. We will remain creatures, albeit everlasting ones, and God will remain God.

There is a view we often hear today — that all human beings are children of God, merely by dint of being born in the image of God. This is clearly not the view of the Beloved Disciple, who says that people become children of God by adoption through faith in Christ. It isn't an inherent condition one is born with. But for those who are Christians the real issue is the struggle to go from being restored in the image to manifesting the actual likeness of God in Christ. And indeed it is often a struggle. Paul speaks of the problems of this struggle when he says in 2 Corinthians 4 that while outwardly we have trials and suffering, inwardly we are being renewed day by day. There is then a tension between our outward form, which is becoming less and less godlike, and our inner self, which is being renewed. Only with the resurrection of believers are the inward and outward finally made commensurate with one another.

We Become What We Admire

Many parents raises their children in such a way that they seek to have their children replicate their own lives or pattern of life. If the father is a doctor, then the son should be a doctor; if the mother went to such and such college then the daughter should as well. This whole process is reinforced by comments like, "He's a real chip off the old block," or, "She's the spitting image of her mother, and has all the same mannerisms too." Children do indeed become what they admire, and often that means becoming like their own parents. But there is another side to this process, a darker side. Sometimes the child strives hard to be like one parent or another, and can never equal or eclipse the parent, and seems doomed to live in the shadow of that parent. The gap between being in the image of the parent, perhaps physically, and being like them in terms of skills or accomplishments is too great to bridge.

How very different this is from what the Beloved Disciple is talking about in 1 John 3. He suggests that God's love reshapes us, not only in conversion, but continually throughout our lives, so that God's perfect love even indwells us and casts out all our fears. And there is an end or *telos* or goal to this loving — full conformity to the image of one's heavenly Father and his messianic Son. Yet it is not only about what God works in us as we make our way towards the resurrection image of Jesus. It is also about what we work out of our lives with fear and trembling.

There is a sense in which our behavior either mars us or helps remake us in God's image. Think of it like a process of polishing a bronze bust. The polish does not make the bust something different nor does it construct or reconstruct the bust, but if the right polish is used, it can make the bust have its brightest and most striking appearance, something glorious rather than dull. In a sense this is what happens when we become imitators of Christ in our behavior. Gradually, between the in-working of God and the process of imitating the One whom we admire, we become more and more like the image of our Maker, or better said, we bear the image more and more clearly. And we should never think that others are not watching to see if we are Christlike persons.

Dr. Fred Douglas was a missionary doctor in Armenia. One day a very sick Moslem was brought into his clinic. Dr. Douglas not only nursed him back to health, but also shared the gospel of Christ with the man. The end result was that the man became a follower of Christ, and took his new-found faith back with him to his native village. Word got out quickly about what had happened, and the man was confronted by the local imam. He confronted the man and said: "All you talk about is Jesus, and yet Jesus died two thousand years ago and you have never even seen him." The man thought for a moment and replied, "I have, in fact, seen Jesus — in Dr.

Douglas. Jesus lives in and is so clearly evident in Dr. Douglas." Imitation, it has been said, is the highest form of flattery.

But if it is true that we become what we admire, then we must be careful about whom we admire, whom we are prepared to count as mentors, whom we choose to follow the example of. In the most recent and last episode of the *Star Wars* saga we find young Anakin Skywalker at a vulnerable point in life. He has been mentored in a wise and good direction by Obi-Wan Kenobi, a Jedi master, but he has also come under the malignant influence of the dark ruler Palpatine. He must choose whom to trust, whom to believe. Whom did he wish to be more like? Unfortunately, he chose to follow the example that led him to the Dark Side of the Force. Behavior, including imitation of a mentor, does indeed lead one either to more closely resemble or more distantly resemble the intended image of God in us all. Discipleship is only a good thing if it is tending towards a good end.

Whose image do people see when they look at you? Are you more like your earthly father or mother, or more like your heavenly Father and his Son? When people look at you — who do they see? It is not enough to be created in the image of God, nor even to be recreated in Christ's image, if you hide or cover up that image in your life. You are on a journey towards full conformity to the image of Christ's Son, both inwardly and outwardly. In that pilgrimage, may we become like the One we admire, and look forward to the day not only when we see him face to face, but when he sees in us, his own image — will we be all we ought to be? Will we hear, "Well done, good and faithful servant; inherit the kingdom"? May we all long and strive for the day when image becomes likeness, the very likeness of love in the person of our true Jedi master — Jesus.

Amen

For Study and Meditation

"What in Creation?"
(Psalm 8)

- Read through Psalm 8 and rewrite it as a personal psalm of praise for the Lord's majesty and sovereignty. If you find such expression difficult, choose another medium to personalize the psalm.
- Meditate on the passage as you spend time outside enjoying God's creation. Take a walk, a hike, or simply sit outside and take in the wonder of creation! Praise God for all that you see.
- Memorize all or part of Psalm 8. Remember that a memorized passage only benefits you as you allow it to take root in your life. Take your time the next few days to memorize these words and write them on your heart.

THOUGHTS FOR FURTHER REFLECTION

"All truth is God's and ultimately leads to God."

Ben Witherington III

"In commanding us to glorify him, God is inviting us to enjoy him."

Oswald Chambers

"You awaken us to delight in Your presence and praises; for You made us for Yourself and our hearts are restless until they find their rest in You."

St. Augustine

"The Supervising Shepherd and the Heavenly Host" (Psalm 23)

+ Pray through Psalm 23. Place yourself in the passage, thanking God for faithfully leading you through all of the circumstances of your life. As you pray through this well-known psalm, take time to pray it for another person as well. Think of the persons in your life who fall along the path described in this passage.
+ Confess to God those times when you have not allowed him to lead you. Often we walk through our lives unaware of the gentle leadership of our Good Shepherd. Ask God to open your eyes to his gentle guidance in your life and thank him for it!
+ Write down your thoughts regarding this passage and sermon. Recount experiences in your life when you have seen God's guiding hand in your life.

THOUGHTS FOR FURTHER REFLECTION

"God has a stake in our lives, and God's honor is affected by how we behave or live our lives precisely because people will look at us and evaluate God on the basis of what they see in us."

Ben Witherington III

"If it is God who leads and feeds you, you will lack for nothing essential throughout life, says the psalmist, especially when it come to God's goodness and mercy or lovingkindness."

Ben Witherington III

"O Good Shepherd, seek me out and bring me home to your fold again. Deal favorably with me according to your grace, 'til I may dwell in your house all the days of my life, and praise you for ever and ever with those who are there. Amen."

St. Jerome (342-420)

"Attempting to Overcome a Tempting"
(1 Corinthians 10:1-13)

◆ Study 1 Corinthians 10:1-13. As you read through the passage, ask yourself what the idols and temptations are in your own life. What keeps you from experiencing God to the fullest?

◆ Pray about the great temptations in your life. Thank God for joining you in your temptations and for always providing a way out. Pray for eyes to see the way out of temptations that befall you.

◆ Fast for the next twenty-four hours from excess noise. You might turn off the music in your car or fast from television, talking on the phone, or the Internet. Use this time to reflect on God's faithfulness in delivering you from temptation.

THOUGHTS FOR FURTHER REFLECTION

"Without God's help we could and will fail and fall."

Ben Witherington III

"God is greater than the scope of our sin or our temptations."

Ben Witherington III

"Thank you, O Lord, that you have promised to be our hiding place no matter what happens."

Corrie ten Boom

For Study and Meditation

"O Lord, let nothing divert our advance towards you, but in this dangerous labyrinth of the world and the whole course of our pilgrimage here, your heavenly dictates be our map and your holy life be our guide."

John Wesley

"We Haven't Got a Prayer"
(Luke 11:1; Matthew 6:5-13)

+ Pray through the Lord's Prayer as it appears in your preferred translation of the Bible. As Christians, we say this prayer quite often. But seldom do we say it slowly enough to soak in the words we are saying. We certainly do not live as though we do. Take each line of the prayer and deliberately, slowly say this well-known prayer.
+ Journal about the Lord's Prayer. You might take it line-by-line tonight (or over several days) and walk through the words. Journal your thoughts on every line. You will never say this prayer the same way again!

THOUGHTS FOR FURTHER REFLECTION

"Prayer is an act of humbling ourselves before our Maker, recognizing that he is in control, and we turn to God not only for help but because we are answerable to God as his creatures."
Ben Witherington III

"Prayer is more than verbally filling in some requisition blank. It's fellowship with God! It is communion with the Lord through praising him, rehearsing his promises, and then sharing our needs."

Billy Graham

"To pray is nothing more involved than to let Jesus into our needs. To pray is to give Jesus permission to apply his power in the alleviation of our distress. To pray is to let Jesus glorify his name in the midst of our needs. To pray is nothing more involved than to open the door, giving Jesus access to our needs and permitting him to exercise his own power in dealing with them."

Ole Hallesby

"Lord, thou knowest what I want, if it be thy will that I should have it. If it be not thy will, Lord, do not be displeased, for I want nothing which thou dost not want for me."

Julian of Norwich

"Pardon, O gracious Jesus, what we have been; with your holy discipline correct what we are. Order by your providence what we shall be; and in the end, crown your own gifts. Amen."

John Wesley

"Lord, take my lips and speak through them, take my mind and think through it, take my heart and set it on fire for love of you."

W. H. Aitken (1841-1927)

"Taxing Situations and Insufferable Self-Centeredness"
(Luke 18:9-14)

- Confess to God those times when you have torn someone else down to build yourself up. Ask God to remind you of your own need for his grace and mercy. Confess those times when you have been quick to judge others by how things appear on the outside. Ask the Lord to give you eyes to see the heart of others and begin praying for the people he has surrounded you with (friends *and* enemies).
- Meditate on Philippians 2:1-11. This hymnic passage is a reminder of the humility of our Savior and the behavior we ought also exhibit. Read the passage at least three times, circling words or phrases that stand out most to you.

◆ Journal the words or phrases that stood out most to you in Philippians 2:1-11. Summarize the passage in your own words for your own life.

◆ Serve another person by committing to pray for them regularly. Find ways to express care for this person and let them know that you are praying for them. Write an encouraging note to this person or do something else to serve them. Often it is in getting outside of ourselves that we are able to see our own need for God's great grace and mercy.

THOUGHTS FOR FURTHER REFLECTION

"Real prayer, the real approach to God, requires not only honesty about self, but it requires the ability and readiness to be self-forgetful, to be willing to sacrifice for others."

Ben Witherington III

"Prayer is not eloquence but earnestness."

Hannah More

"Real prayer is taking His word into the Throne Room and letting His words speak through your lips to Him on the throne, calling His attention to His own promises."

E. W. Kenyon

"From Image to Likeness"
(1 John 3:2)

◆ Memorize 1 John 3:1-3. Allow these encouraging words to take root in your heart and soul. Writing this passage on the tablet of your heart will encourage and challenge you. It will encourage you as you remember God's promises for the future. It will challenge you to live as one made in the image of your God.

◆ Worship God for creating you in his image. You might read the creation narrative in Genesis 1 and our passage during your time of worship.

Choose hymns or praise songs to sing or listen to that give God praise for the way he has created us.

- Pray for strength to be who God created you to be. Confess to God where you have danced for men's eyes and covered up his image in your life. Pray for a renewed energy to live wholly and completely for him. Ask him to remold and make you into a person that reflects his image.

Thoughts for Further Reflection

"Discipleship is only a good thing if is tending towards a good end."

Ben Witherington III

"It is not enough to be created in the image of God, nor even to be re-created in Christ's image, if you hide or cover up that image in your life."

Ben Witherington III

"God hasn't given up on you. He can still do great things for you, in you, and through you. God is ready and waiting and able."

Peter Marshall